AUTHENTIC TRANSCRIPTIONS
WITH NOTES AND TABLATURE

# BECK SEA CHANGE

T0045178

## CONTENTS

Music transcriptions by Andrew Moore, David Stocker, and Jeff Story

ISBN 0-634-06309-X

7777 W. BLUEMOUND RD. P.O. BOX 13819 MILWAUKEE, WI 53213

Visit Hal Leonard Online at
**www.halleonard.com**

# The Golden Age

**Words and Music by Beck Hansen**

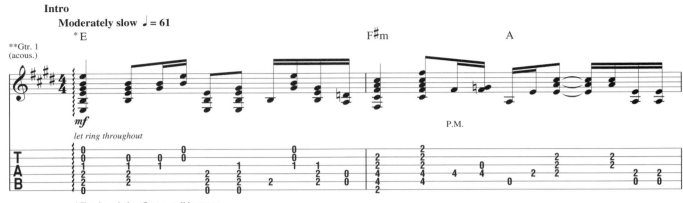

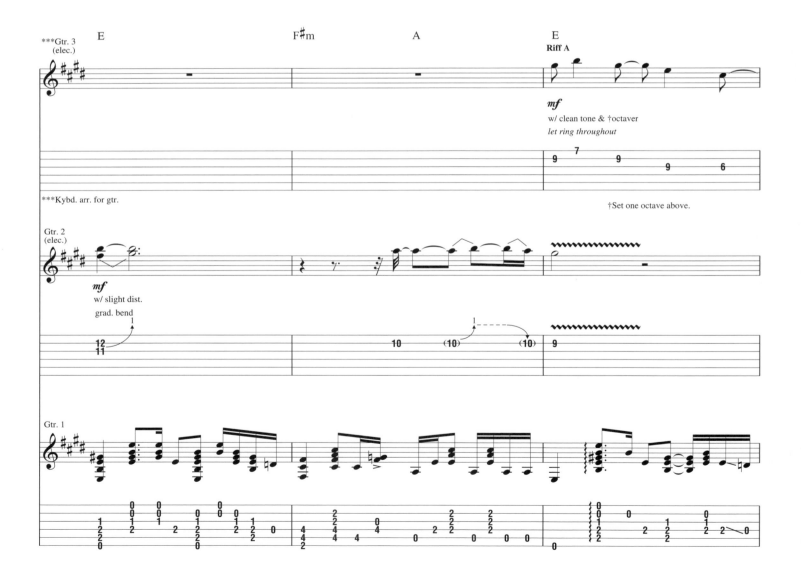

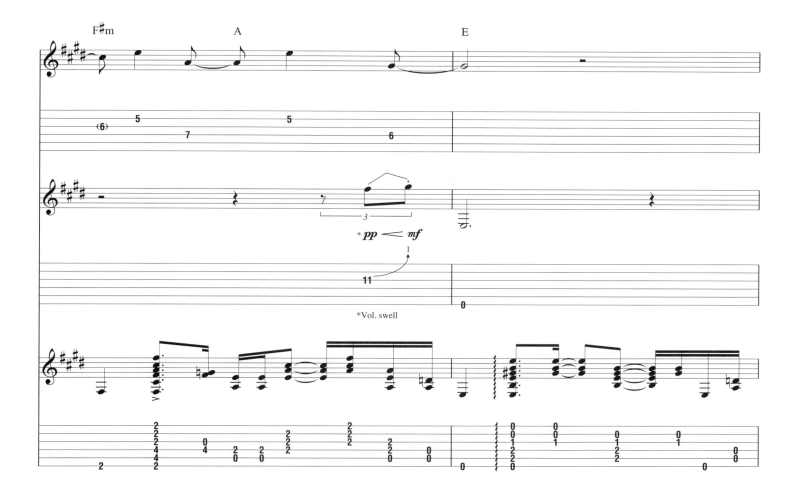

Gtr. 3: w/ Riff A

End Riff A

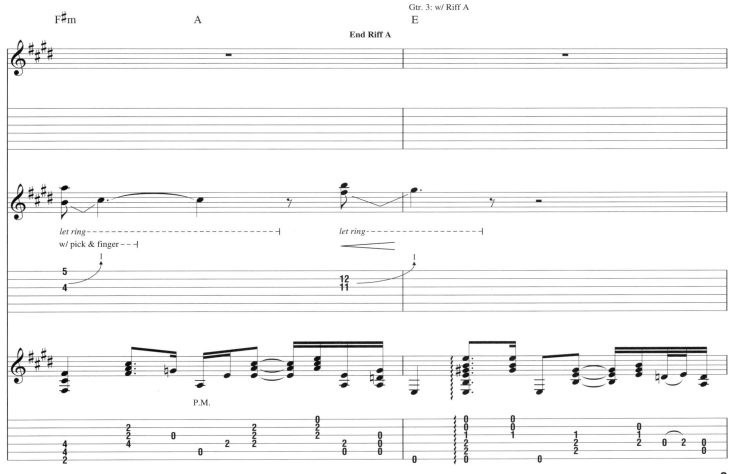

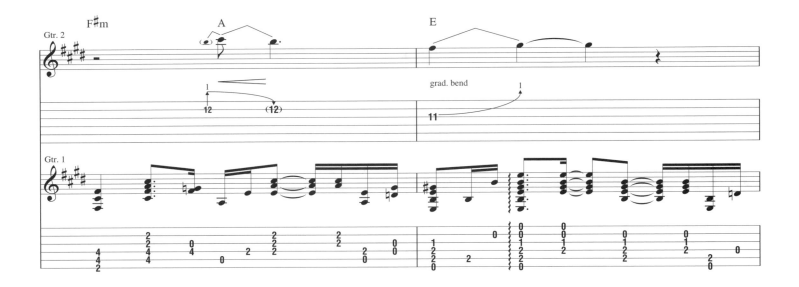

**Verse**

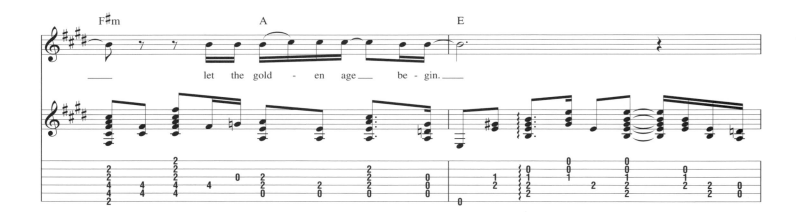

1. Put your hands on the wheel, ____

let the gold - en age ____ be - gin. ____

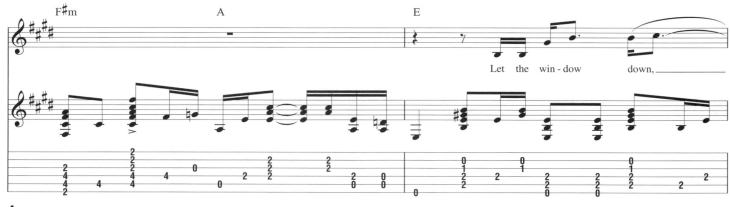

Let the win - dow down, ____

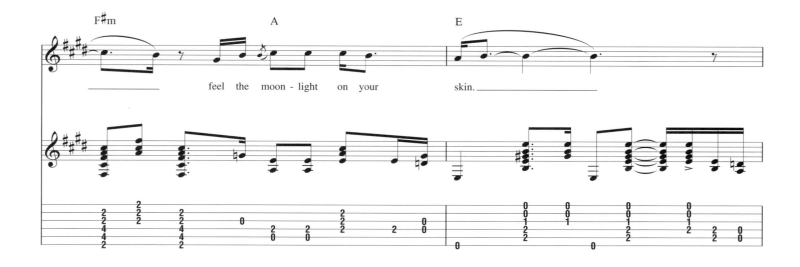

feel the moon - light    on your        skin.

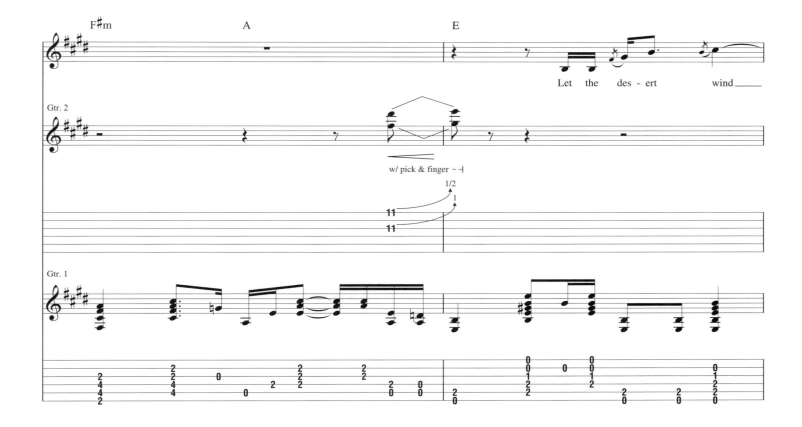

Gtr. 2

w/ pick & finger

Let   the   des - ert   wind

Gtr. 1

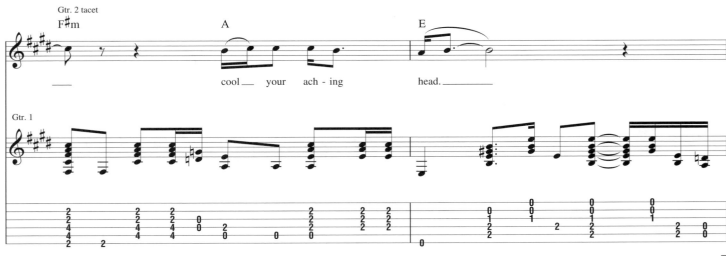

Gtr. 2 tacet

cool___ your   ach - ing        head.___

Gtr. 1

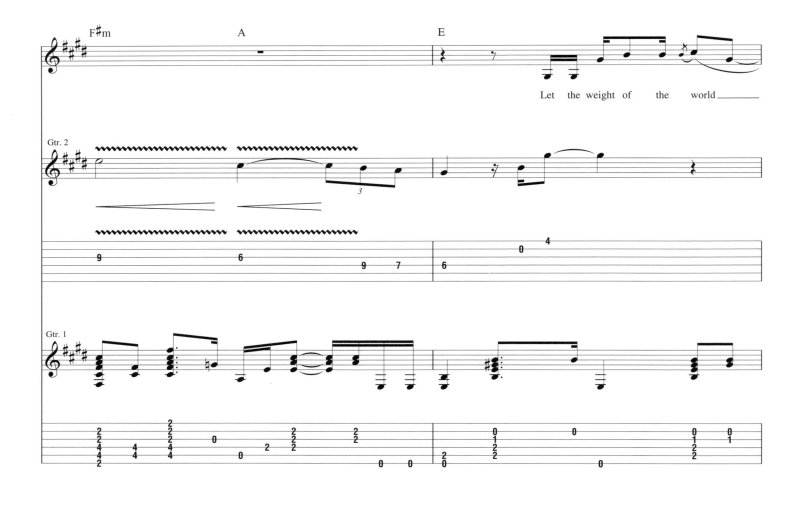

Let the weight of the world _____

____ drift a - way ___ in - stead. _____

w/ pick & finger
*let ring - - - -*

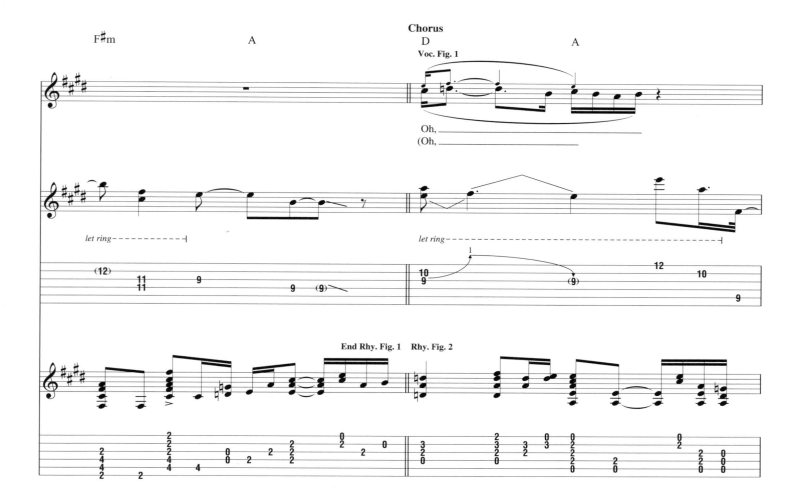

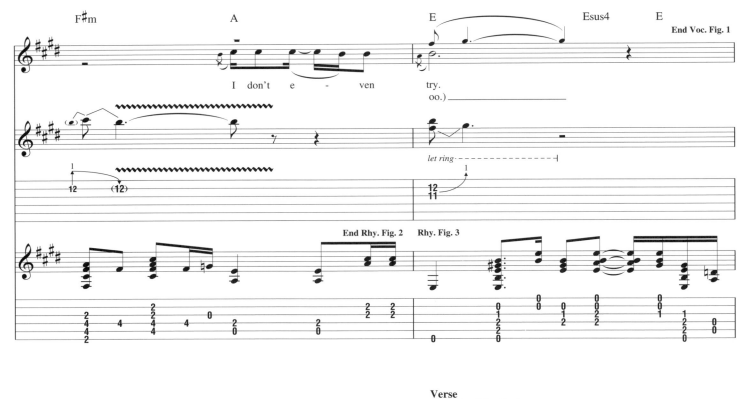

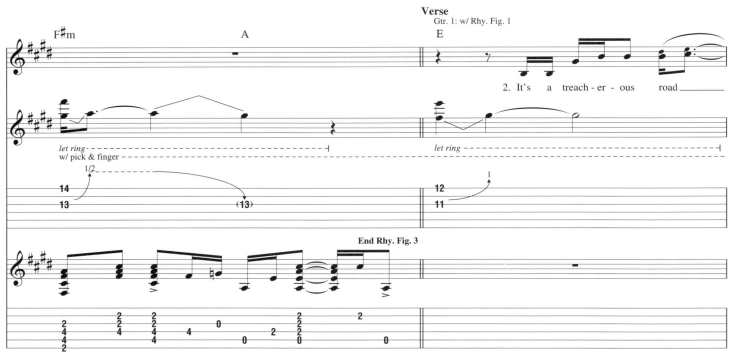

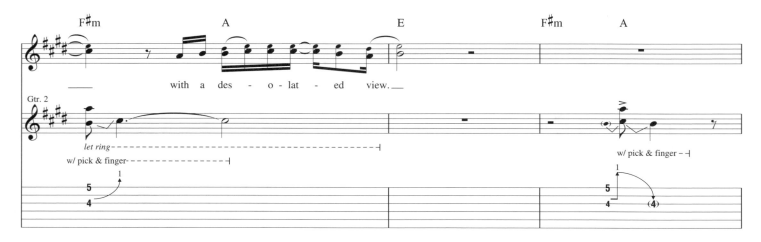

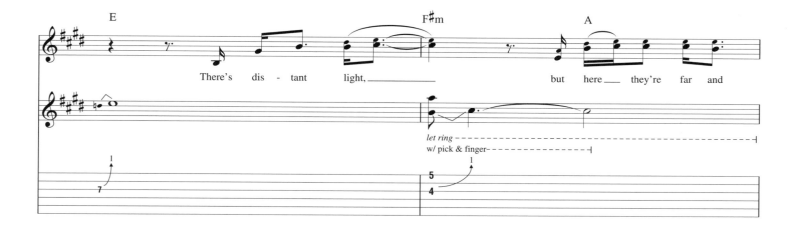

There's dis - tant light, _____ but here \_\_\_ they're far and

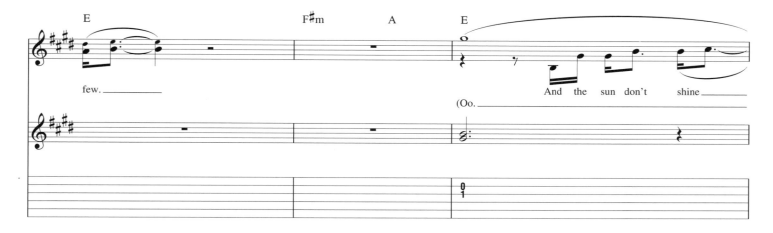

few. _____ And the sun don't shine _____

(Oo. _____

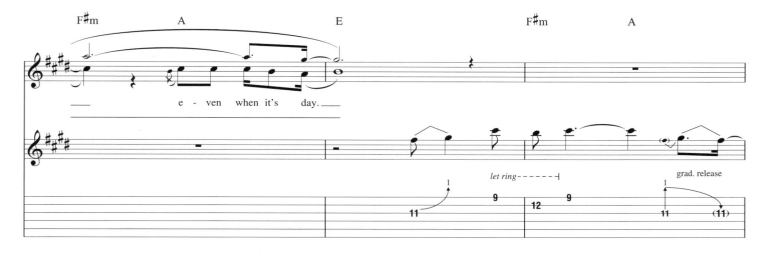

\_\_\_ e - ven when it's day. \_\_\_

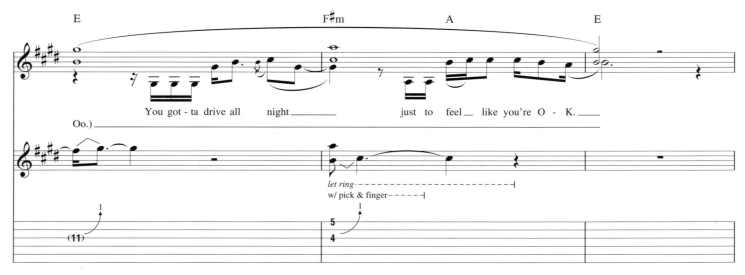

You got - ta drive all night _____ just to feel \_\_\_ like you're O - K. \_\_\_

Oo.)

**Chorus**

Bkgd. Voc.: w/ Voc. Fig. 1
Gtr. 1: w/ Rhy. Fig. 2

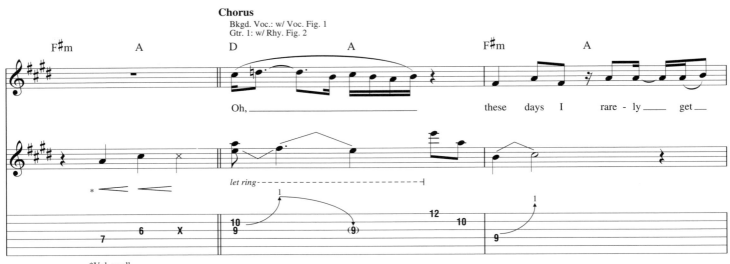

*Vol. swell

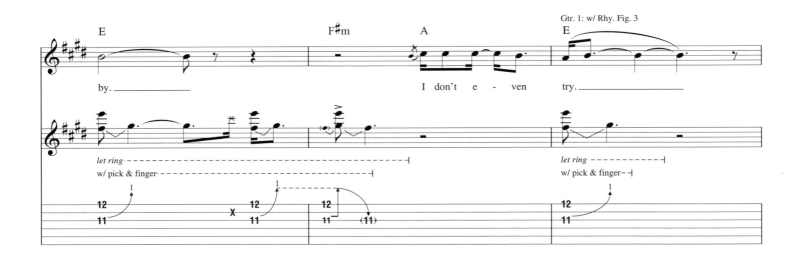

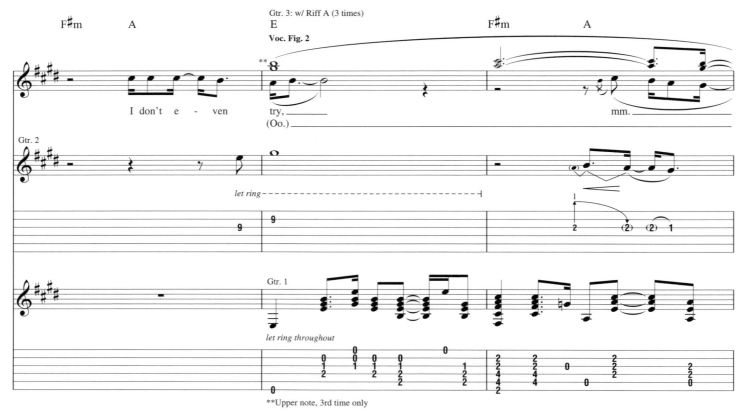

**Upper note, 3rd time only

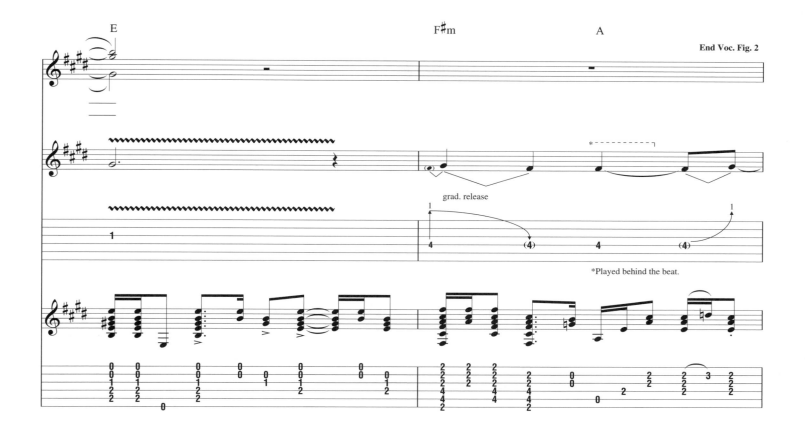

*Played behind the beat.

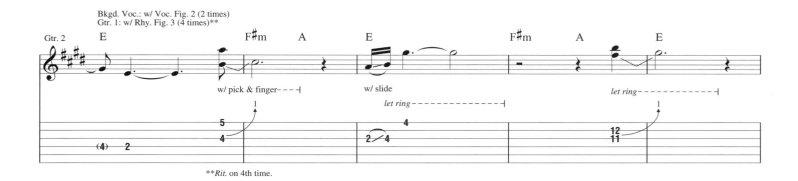

Bkgd. Voc.: w/ Voc. Fig. 2 (2 times)
Gtr. 1: w/ Rhy. Fig. 3 (4 times)**

**Rit. on 4th time.

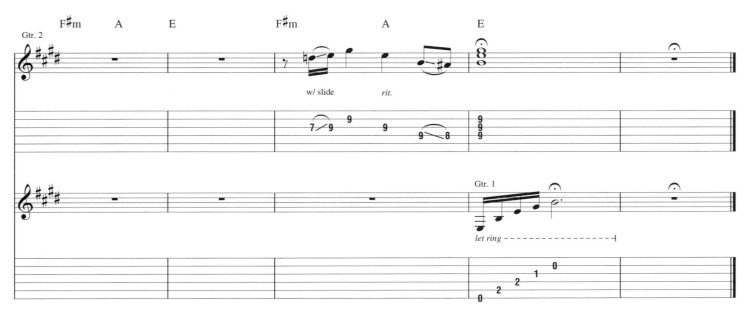

# Paper Tiger

**Words and Music by Beck Hansen**

That all the laws of cre - a - tion _____ that tell a dead _ man how to die. _____

**Chorus**

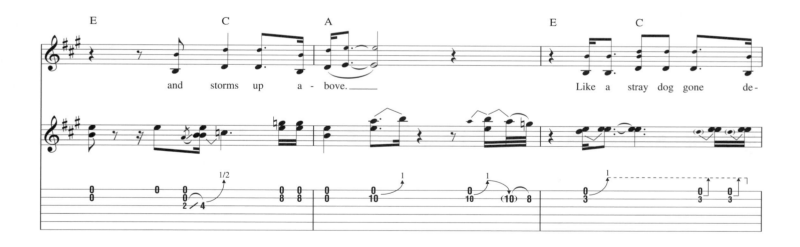

Oh, des - erts down be - low us _____ and storms up a - bove. _____ Like a stray dog gone de -

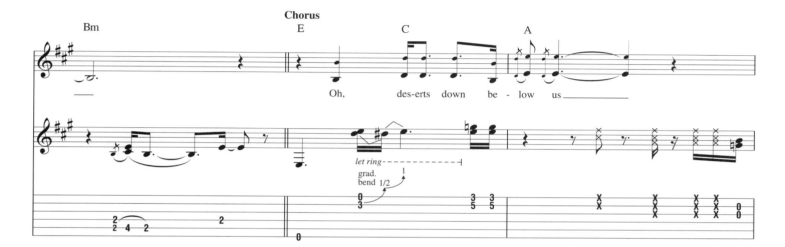

fec - tive, _____ like a pa - per _____ ti - ger _____ in the

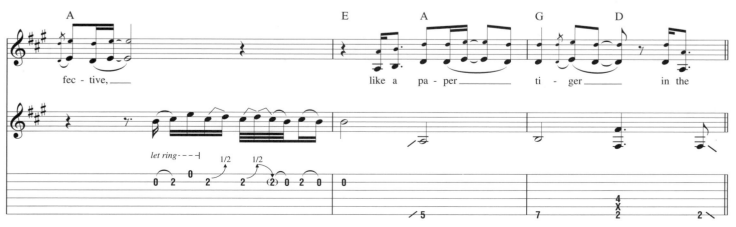

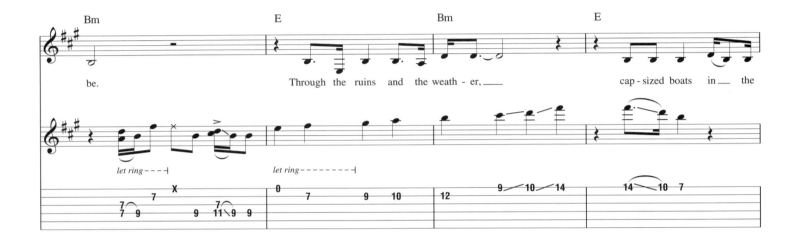

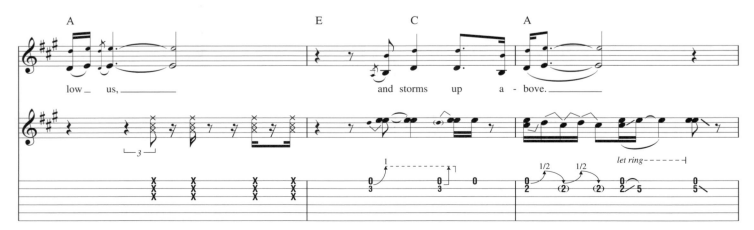

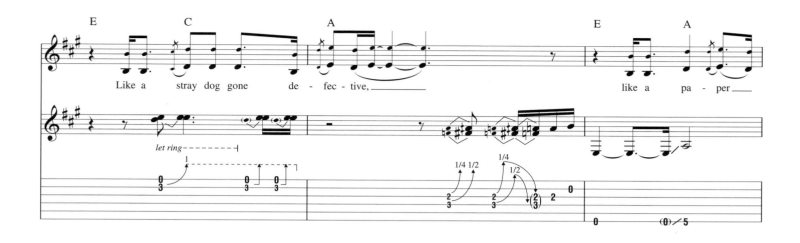

Like a stray dog gone de - fec - tive,                    like a pa - per

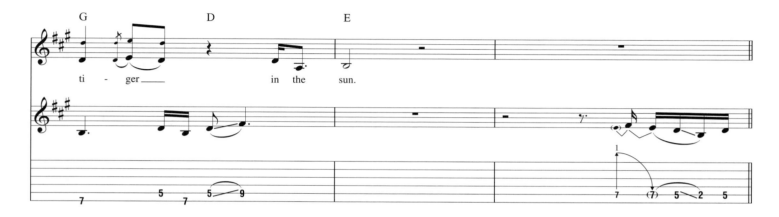

ti - ger          in the sun.

**Bridge**

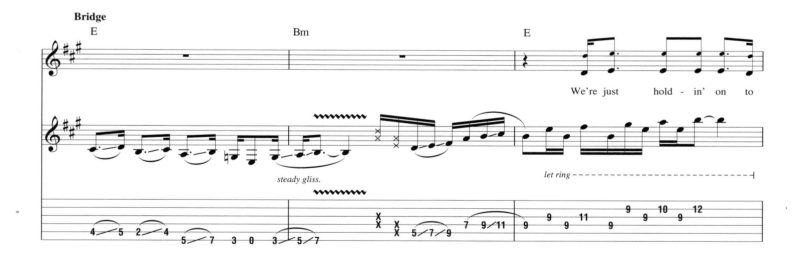

We're just        hold - in' on to

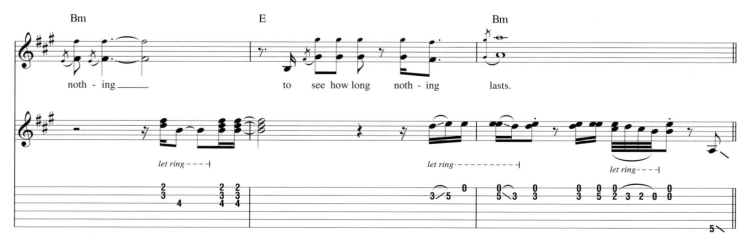

noth - ing          to   see how long   noth - ing      lasts.

**Chorus**

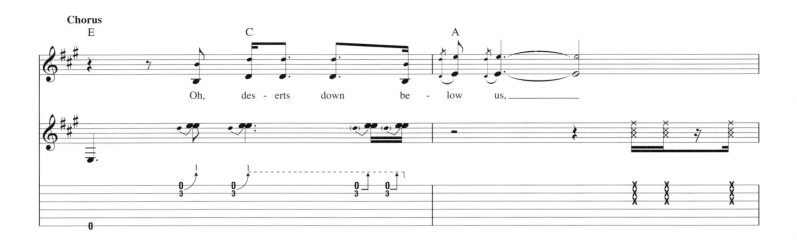

Oh, des - erts down be - low us, ___

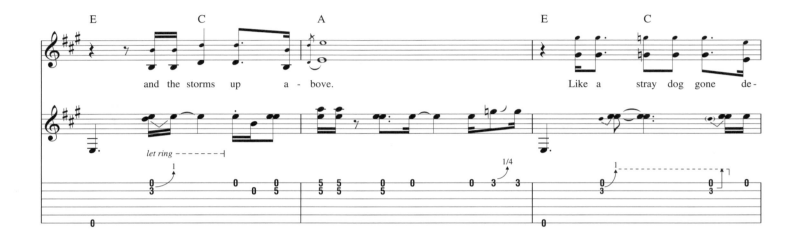

and the storms up a - bove. Like a stray dog gone de-

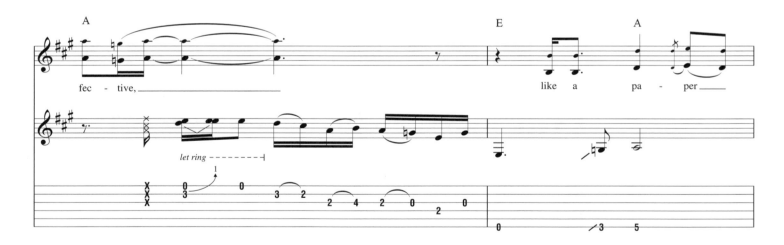

fec - tive, ___ like a pa - per ___

**Guitar Solo**

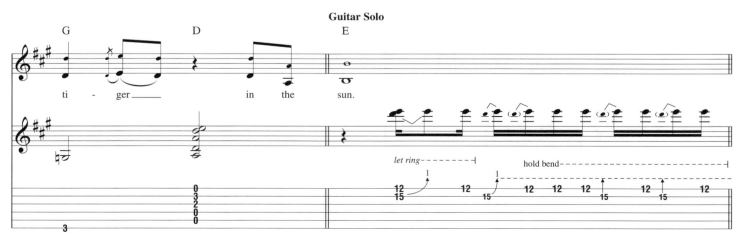

ti - ger ___ in the sun.

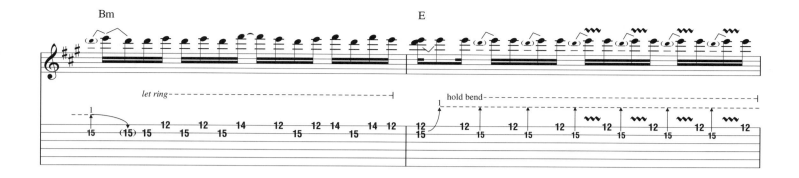

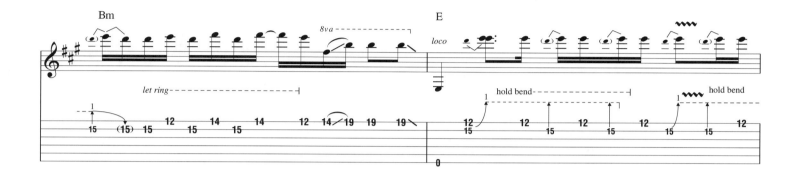

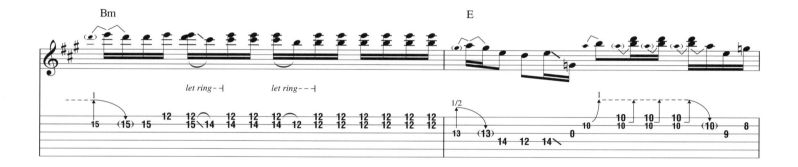

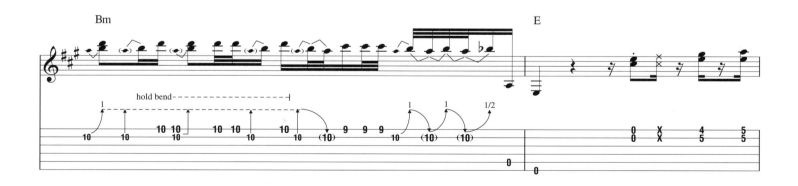

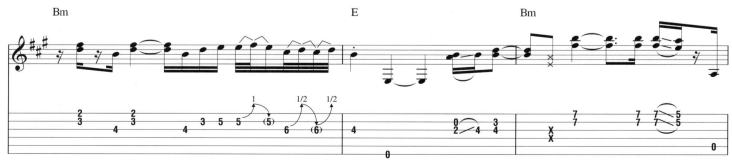

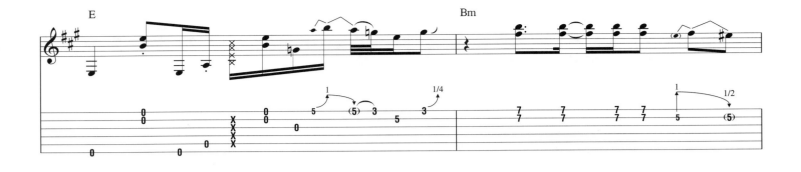

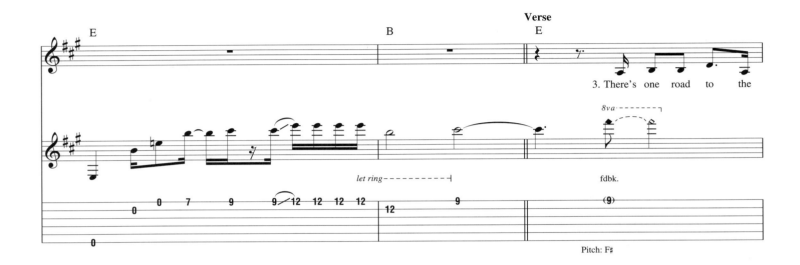

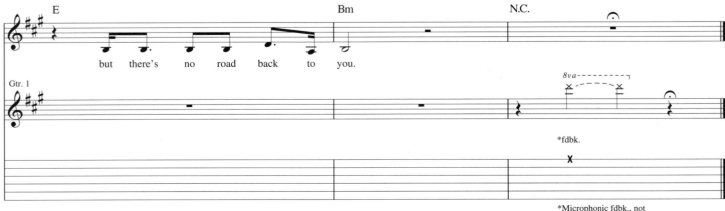

# Guess I'm Doing Fine

**Words and Music by Beck Hansen**

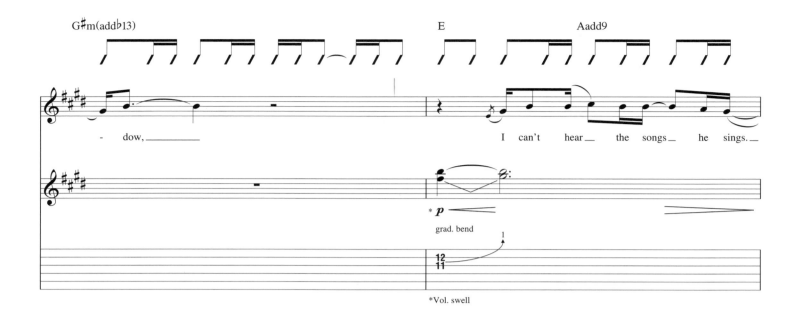

- dow, _____

I can't hear_ the songs_ he sings.

*p* grad. bend

*Vol. swell

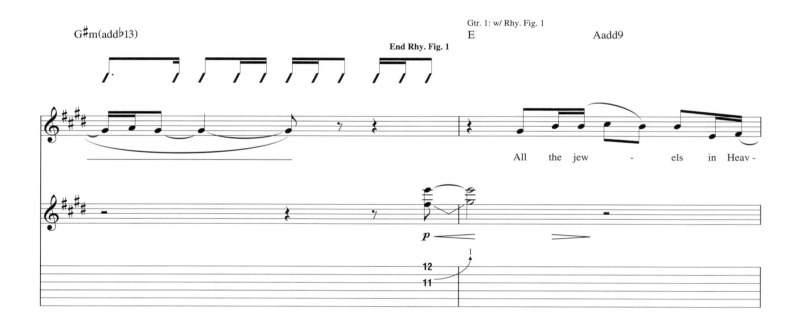

Gtr. 1: w/ Rhy. Fig. 1

End Rhy. Fig. 1

All the jew - els in Heav -

*p*

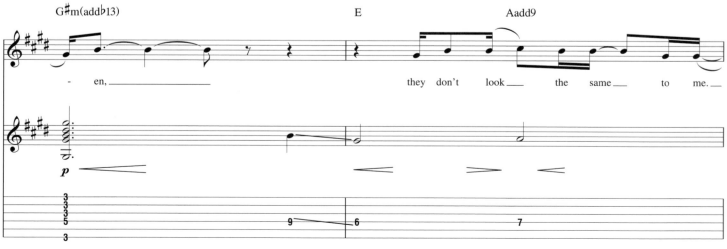

- en, _____

they don't look_ the same_ to me. _

*p*

G#m(add♭13)                    G6                    Aadd9

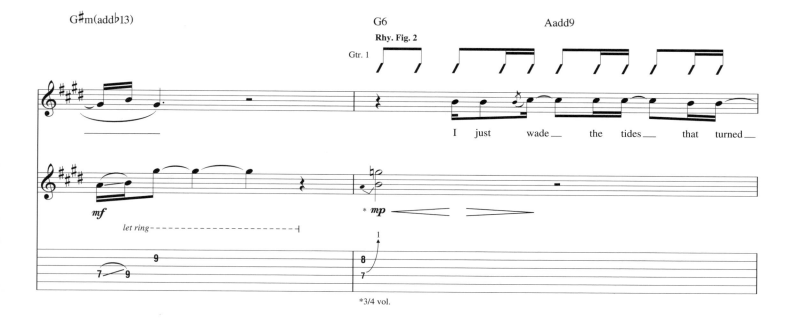

I just    wade___ the tides___ that turned___

*3/4 vol.

G6                F#m11                E                    End Rhy. Fig. 2

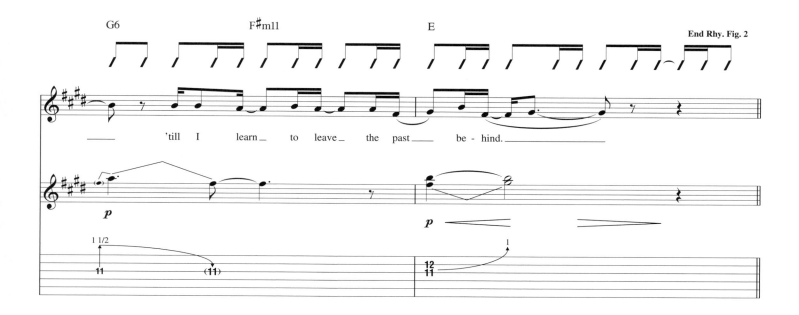

___ 'till I   learn___ to leave___ the past___ be - hind._____

**Pre-Chorus**
G#m(add♭13)              Aadd9                E

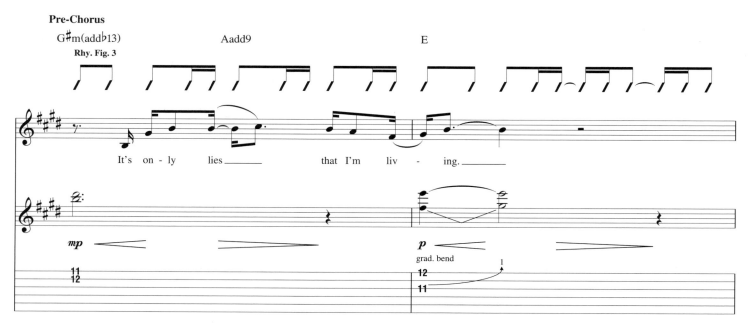

It's on - ly lies_____ that I'm liv - ing.

**21**

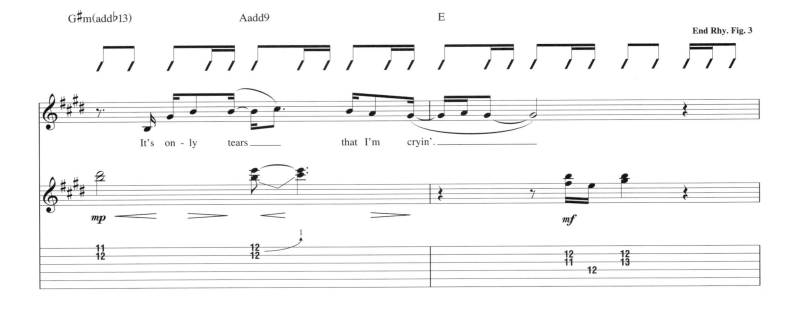

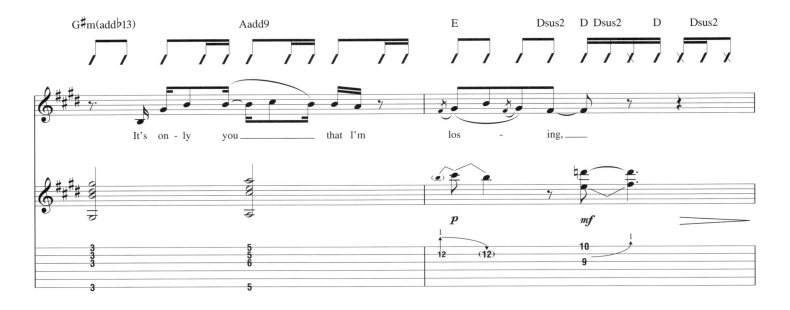

22

**Verse**

2. All the bat - tle - ments ___ are emp - ty, ___

and the moon ___ is lay - in' low. ___ Yel - low ros - es in the grave -

*Clavinet arr. for gtr.

**Pre-Chorus**

Gtr. 1: w/ Rhy. Fig. 3
Gtr. 3 tacet

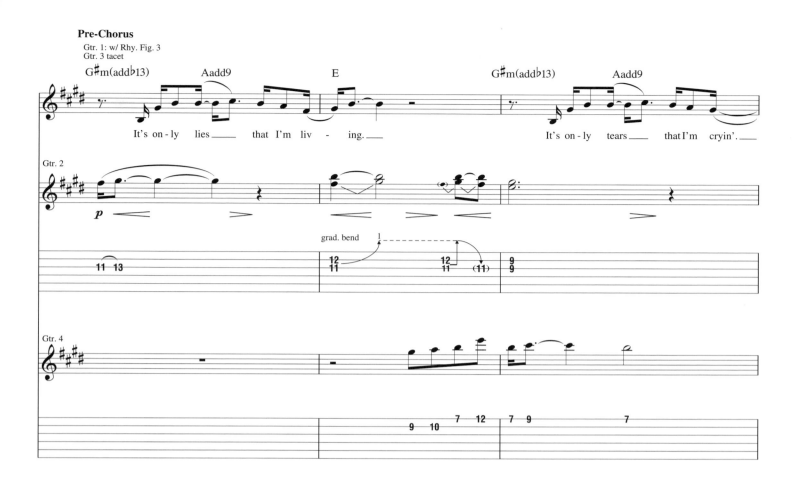

It's on-ly lies ____ that I'm liv - ing. ____          It's on-ly tears ____ that I'm cryin'. ____

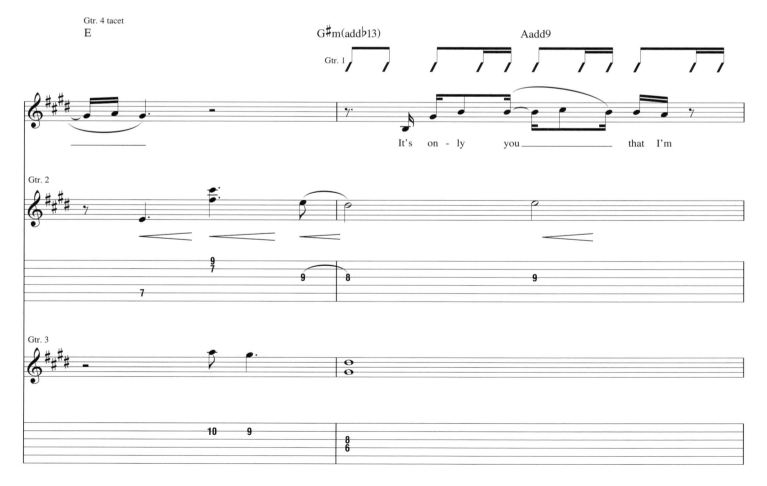

It's on-ly you _____ that I'm

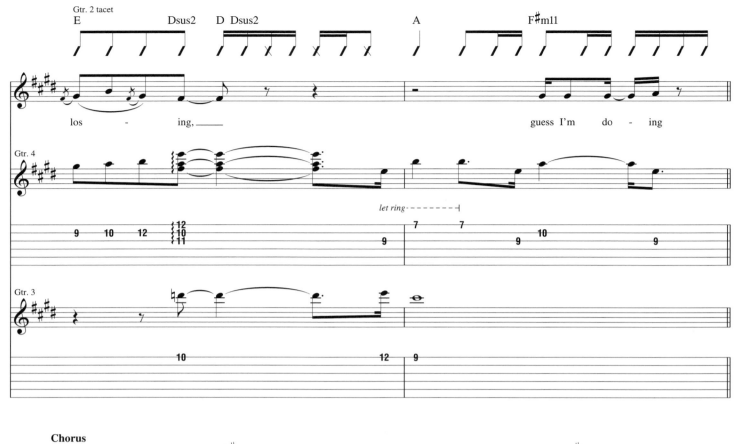

los - ing, _____ guess I'm do - ing

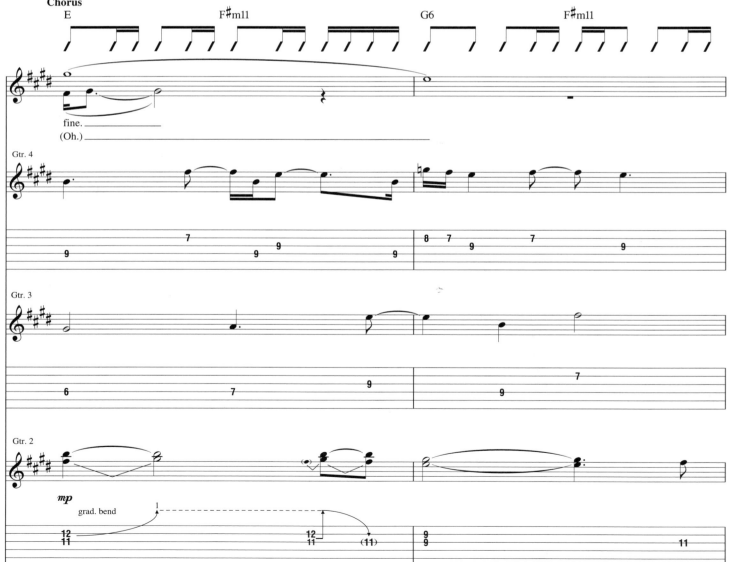

**Chorus**

fine. _____

(Oh.) _____

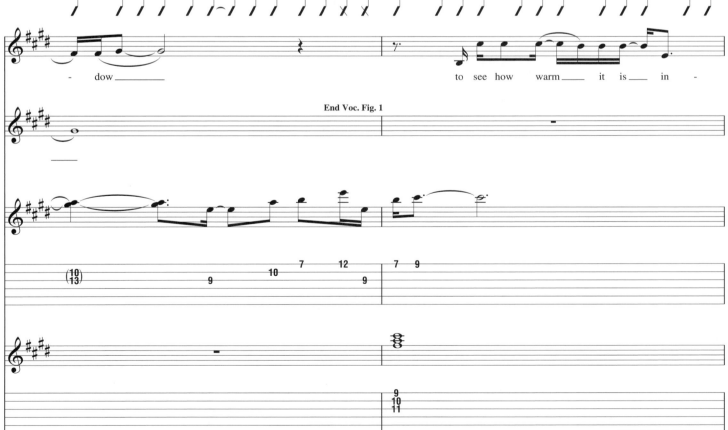

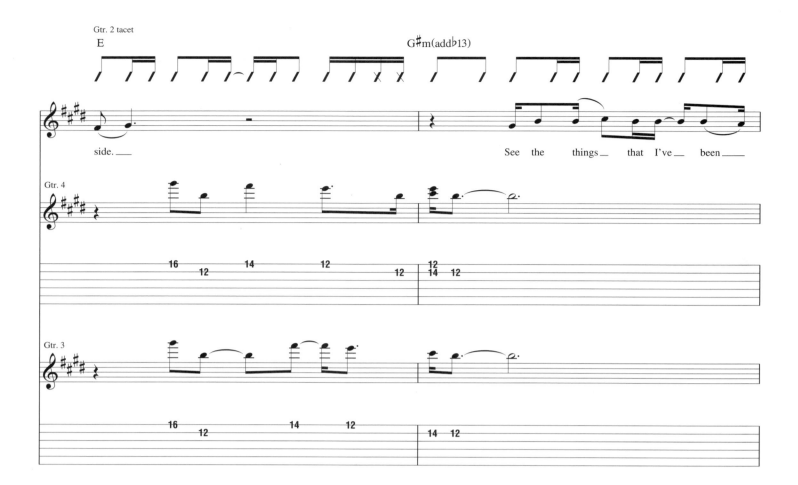

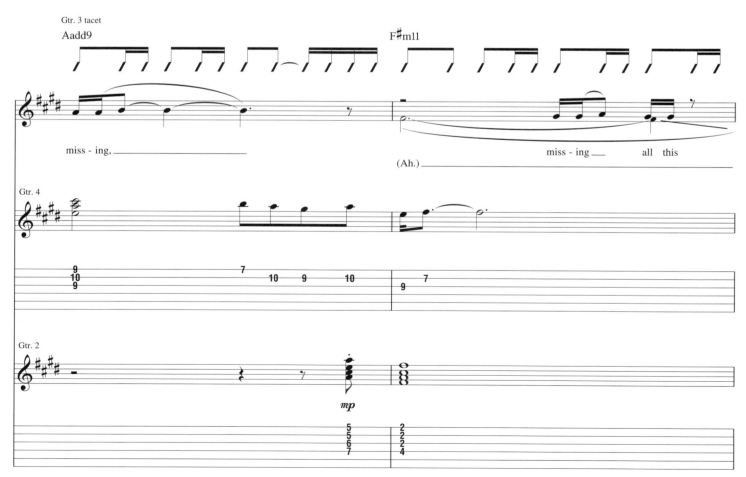

**Pre-Chorus**

Gtr. 1: w/ Rhy. Fig. 3

Gtr. 4 tacet

E    G#m(add♭13)    Aadd9

time. _____

Gtr. 2

It's on-ly lies _____ that I'm

*mf*

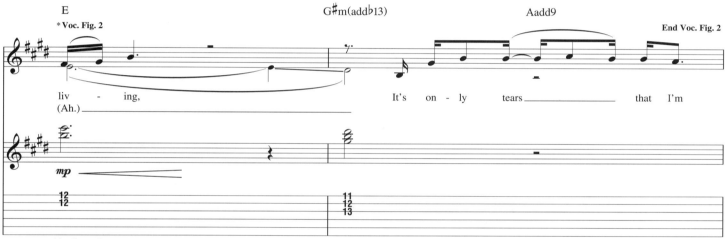

E    G#m(add♭13)    Aadd9    End Voc. Fig. 2

*Voc. Fig. 2

liv- ing,
(Ah.) _____

It's on-ly tears _____ that I'm

*mp*

*Applies to downstem notes only.

Bkgd. Voc.: w/ Voc. Fig. 2

E    G#m(add♭13)    Aadd9

Gtr. 1

cryin'. _____

It's on-ly you _____ I'm

Gtr. 4

*8va* ------- *loco*

Gtr. 2

29

30

**Outro**

# Lonesome Tears

## Words and Music by Beck Hansen

*Chord symbols reflect basic harmony.

for.            Oh,___ they ru - in me ___ ev - 'ry ___ time.

But I'll ___ try _____ to leave be - hind___ some___ days _____

these tears just can't e - rase,        I don't need___ them an - y -

**%  Chorus**

more.                                    How could this ___ love, ___

ev - er turn - ing, ___            nev - er turn ___ it's eye ___ on ___ me? ___

How could this ___ love, ___   ev - er chang - ing, ___   nev - er change ___ the way I ___ feel? ___

*To Coda* ⊕

# Lost Cause

**Words and Music by Beck Hansen**

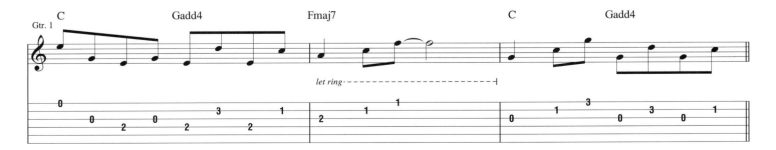

**Verse**

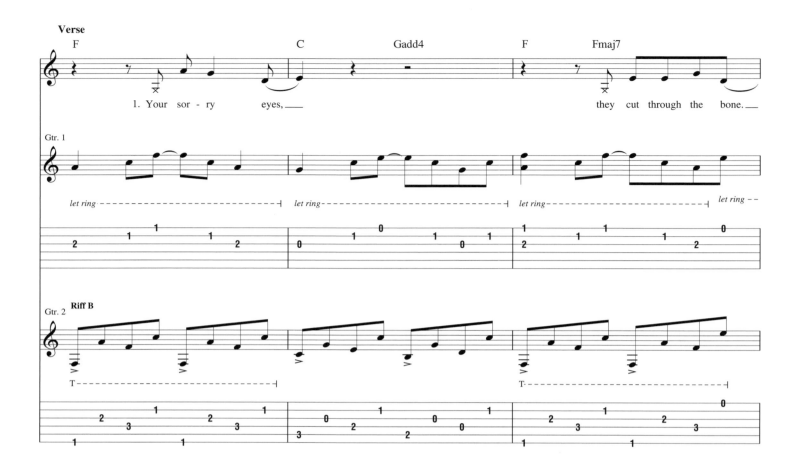

1. Your sor - ry eyes, _____ they cut through the bone. \_\_\_

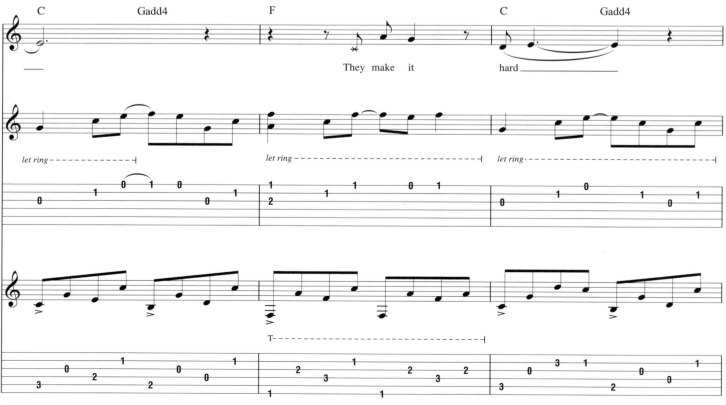

They make it hard _____

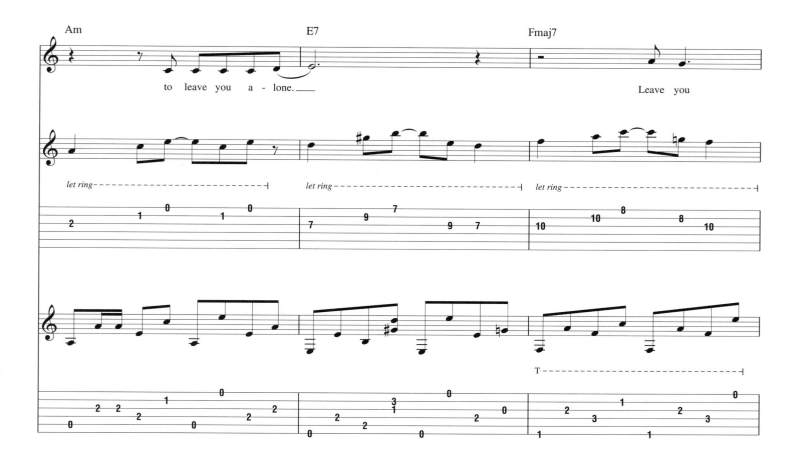

to leave you a - lone. ___ Leave you

here ___ wear - in' your wounds, ___

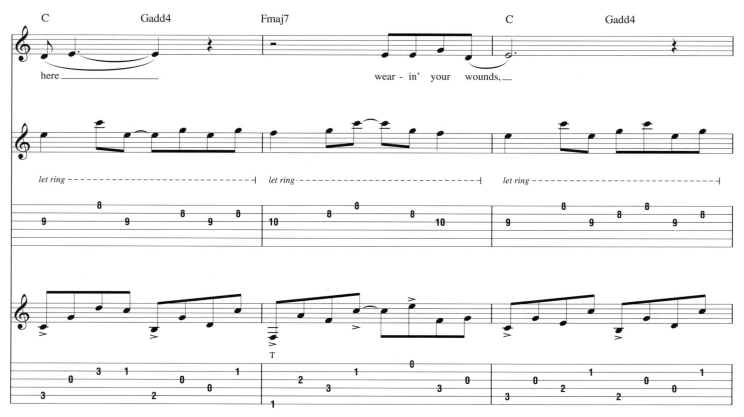

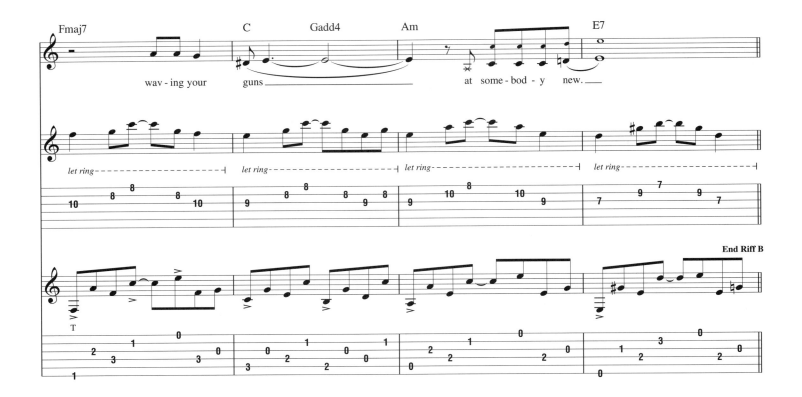

wav - ing your guns _____ at some - bod - y new. ___

**End Riff B**

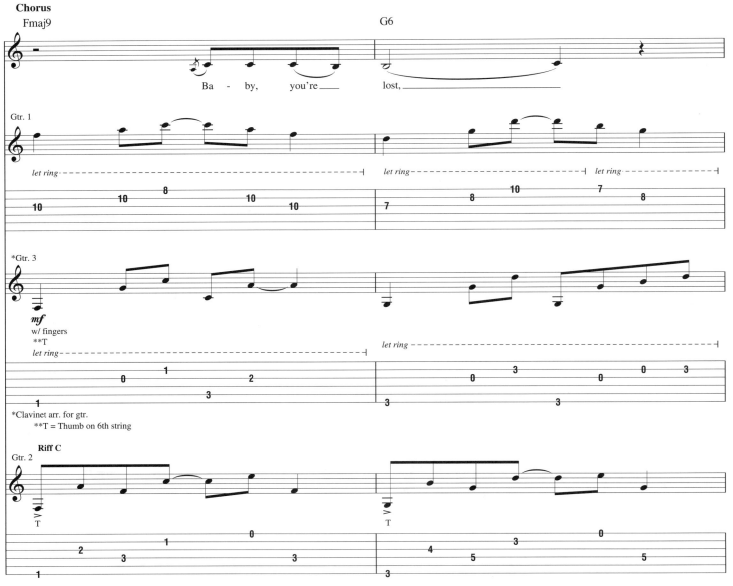

**Chorus**

Ba - by, you're ___ lost, _____

Gtr. 1

*Gtr. 3

*mf*
w/ fingers
**T
*let ring*

*Clavinet arr. for gtr.
**T = Thumb on 6th string

**Riff C**
Gtr. 2

**Verse**

Gtr. 2: w/ Riff B
Gtr. 3 tacet

2. There's too man - y peo - ple             you used to know.

Gtr. 1

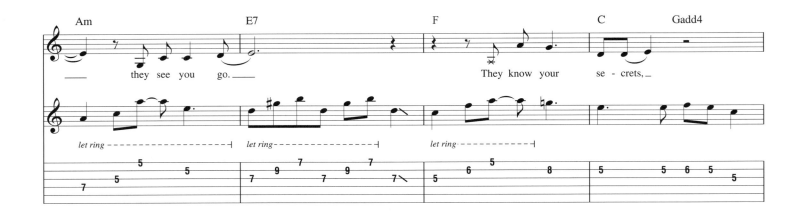

They see you       com - in',

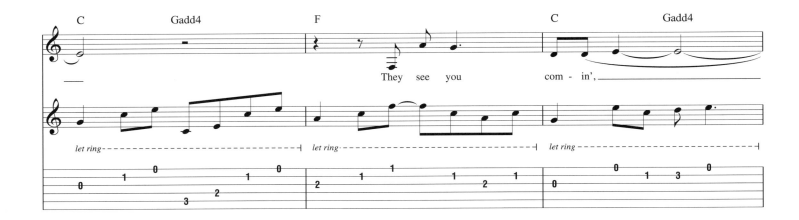

they see you go.                 They know your      se - crets,

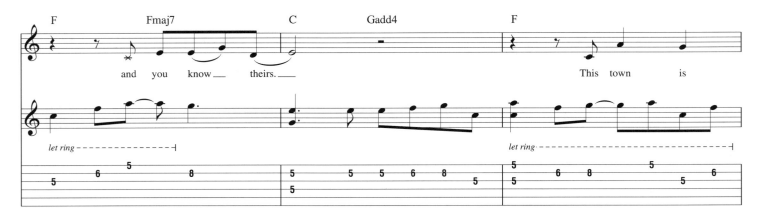

and you know   theirs.                      This town is

**Chorus**

Gtr. 2: w/ Riff C

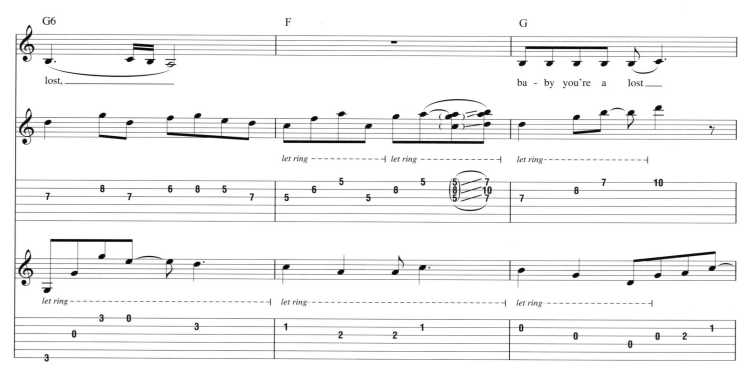

That's what you ___ thought love ___ was ___

(Oo.) ___

for. ___

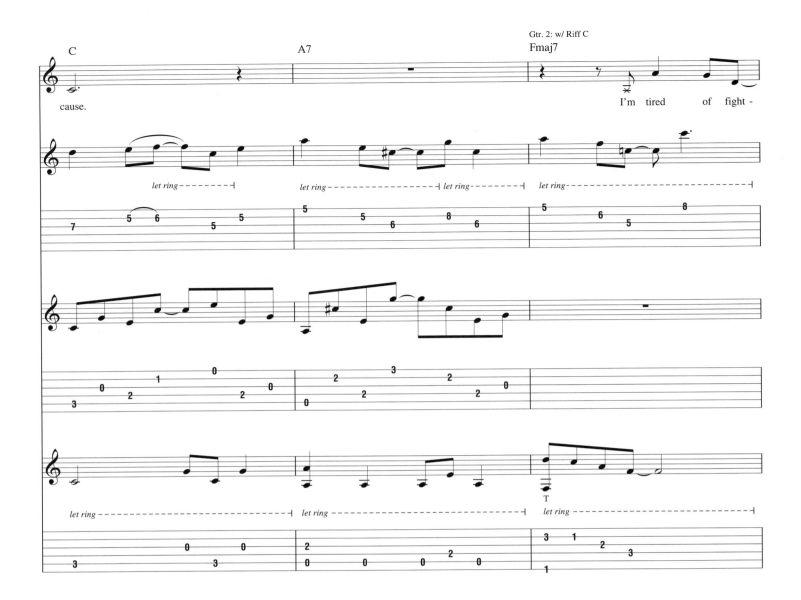

# End of the Day

### Words and Music by Beck Hansen

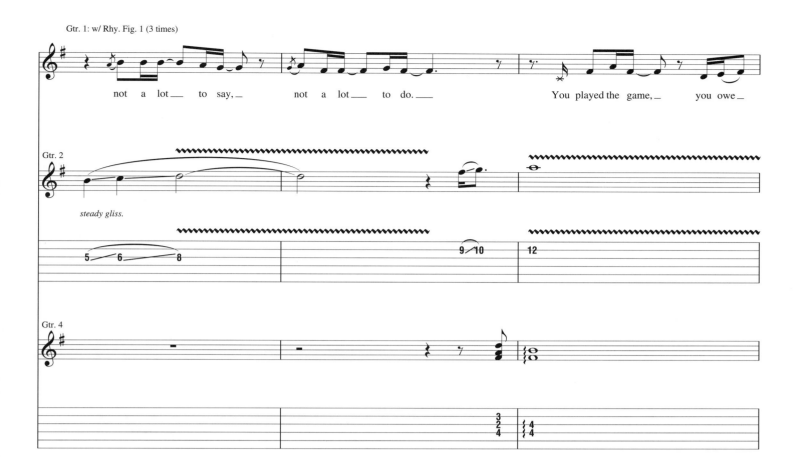

**Interlude**

\* Synthesizer arr. for gtr.

**Verse**

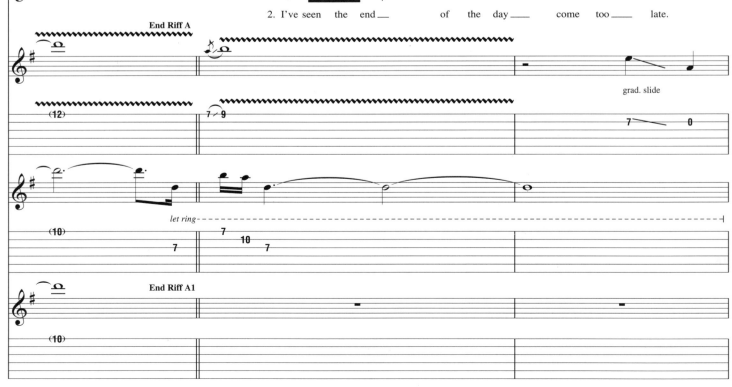

Seen the love_ you had_ turn - ing in - to_ hate.      Had to act_ like I

did-n't e - ven_ care,      but I did so, I_ got strand-ed stand-ing_ there,      stand-ing_

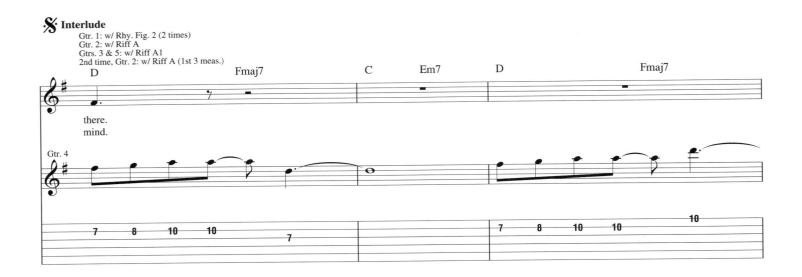

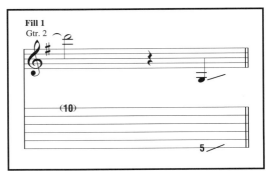

still ____ kills ____ me like it ____ did ____ be - fore. No, it's ____ noth-ing ____ that I have-n't

*To Coda* ⊕

seen be - fore, ____ but it still ____ kills ____ me like it ____ did ____ be - fore. ____

*let ring*

*let ring*

55

**Interlude**
Gtr. 5 tacet
Gmaj7/D

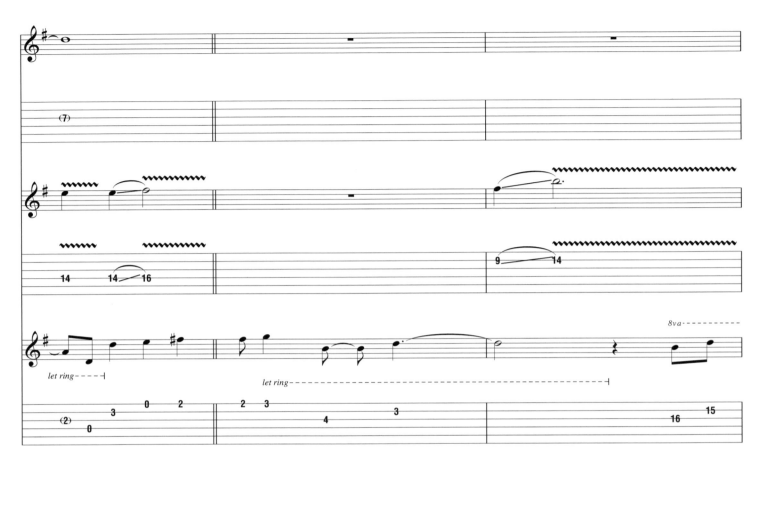

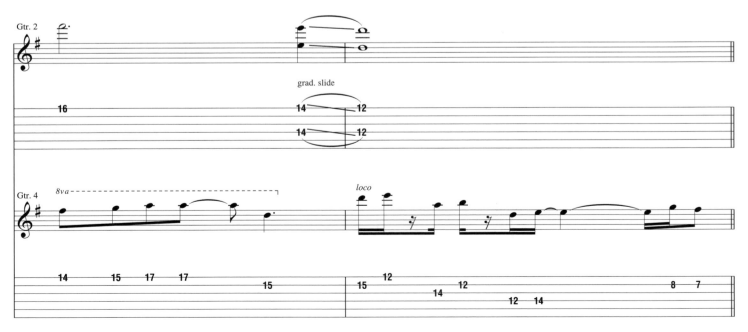

**Verse**

Gtr. 1: w/ Rhy. Fig. 1 (4 times)    Gtr. 5 tacet

Gmaj7/D

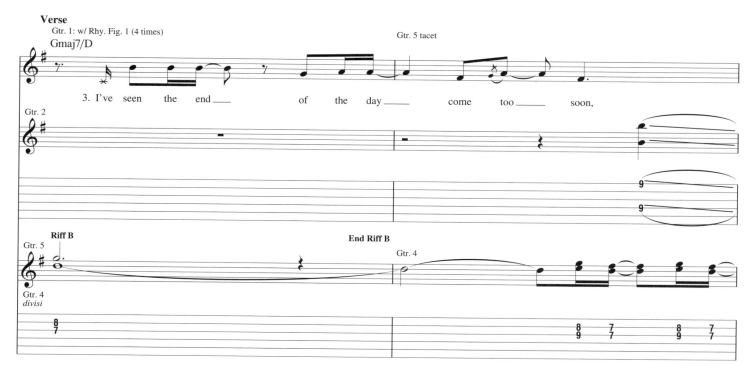

3. I've seen the end ___ of the day ___ come too ___ soon,

like the pris - on dogs ___ they sent out af - ter ___ you. You owe noth - ing to the past ___

___ but wast-ed ___ time to serve a sen - tence that was on - ly in your mind, in your

* Pluck top note only.

**D.S. al Coda**

57

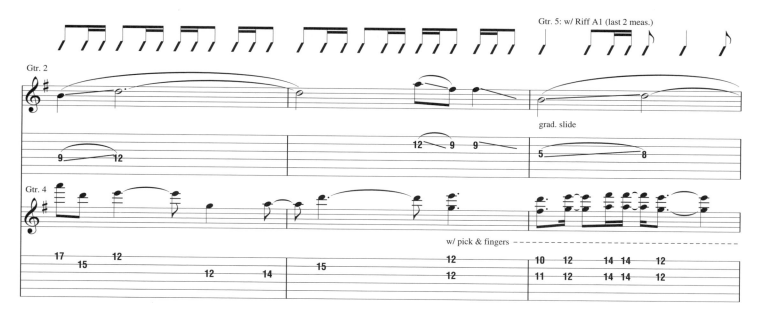

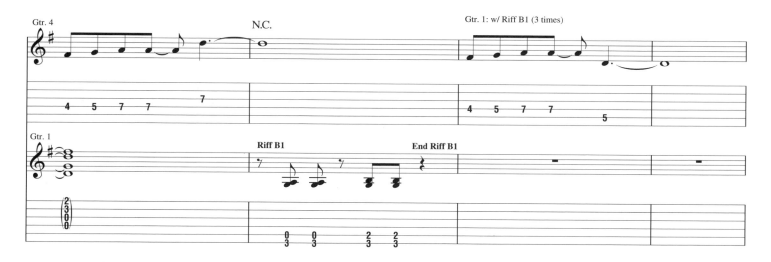

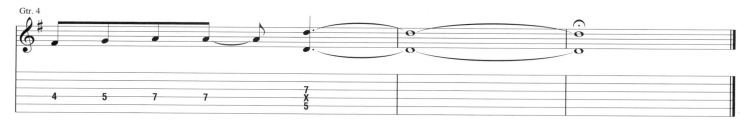

# All in Your Mind
## (It's All in Your Mind)

**Words and Music by Beck Hansen**

*Cello & bass arr. for gtr.

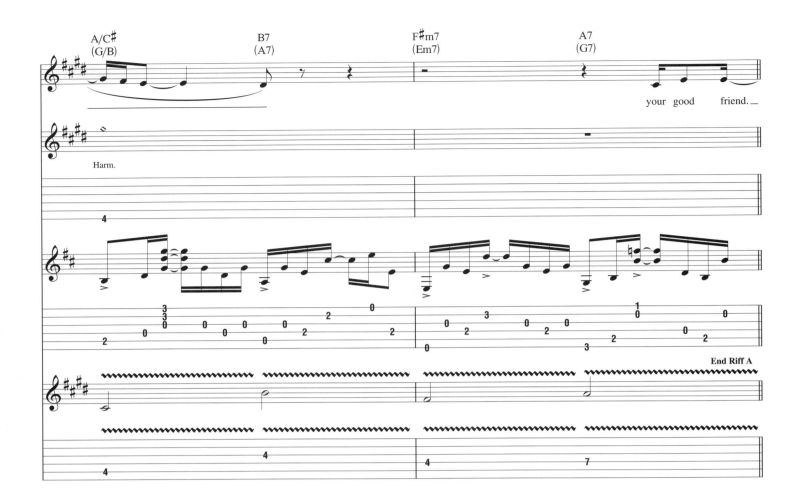

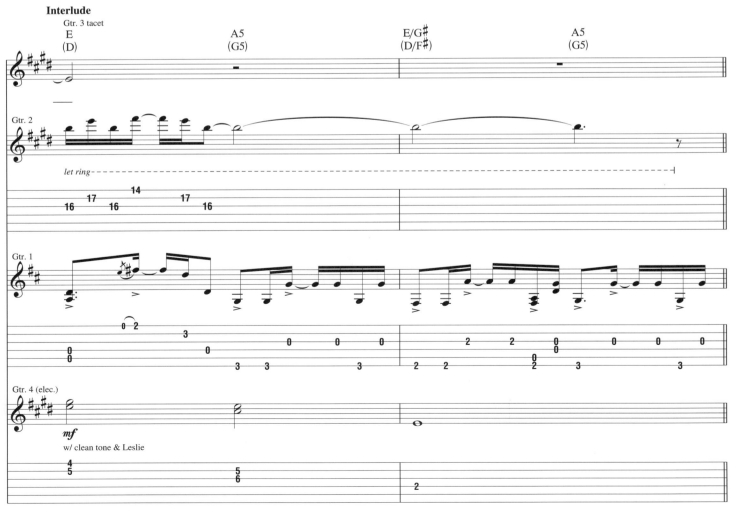

64

# Round the Bend

**Words and Music by Beck Hansen**

**Interlude**

Gtr. 1: w/ Rhy. Fig. 1

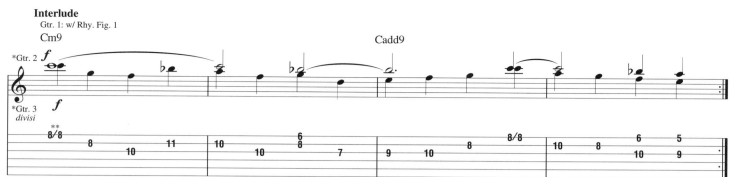

*Strings arr. for gtr.

　**Gtr. 3 to left of slash in tab.

Gtr. 1: w/ Rhy. Fig. 1

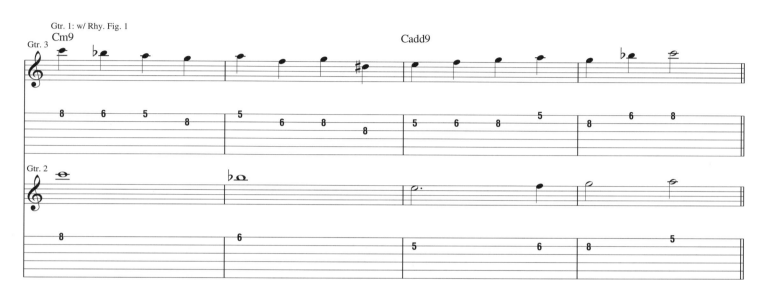

**Outro**

Gtr. 1: w/ Rhy. Fig. 1

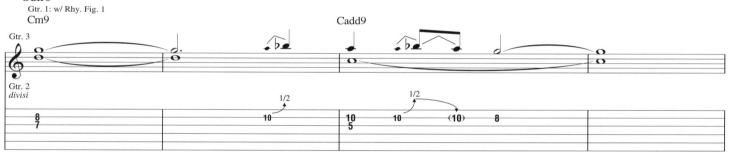

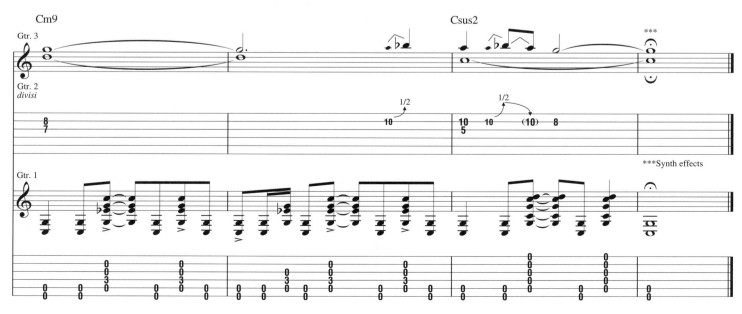

***Synth effects

# Already Dead

**Words and Music by Beck Hansen**

Open G tuning:
(low to high) D-G-D-G-B-D

**Intro**

**Slowly** ♩ = 58

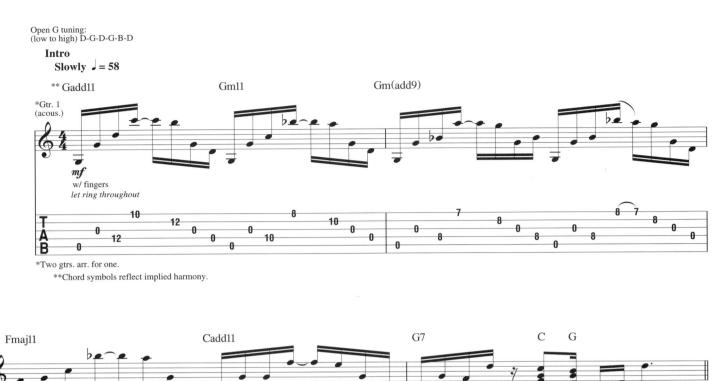

*Two gtrs. arr. for one.
**Chord symbols reflect implied harmony.

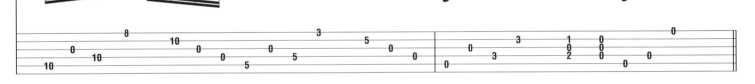

**Verse**

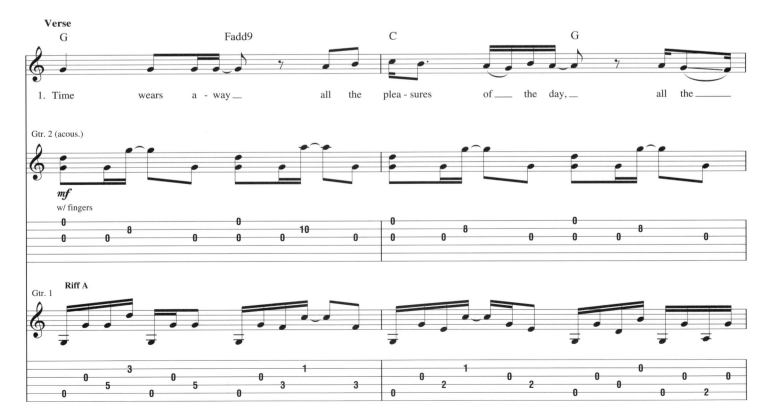

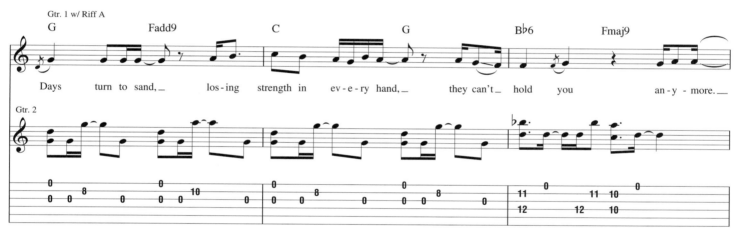

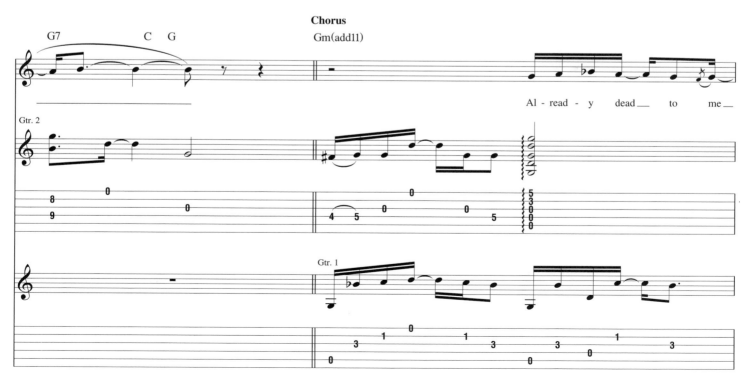

Gm6add11

now, _____ al - read - y dead \_\_ to \_\_ me \_\_ now. _____ 'Cause it

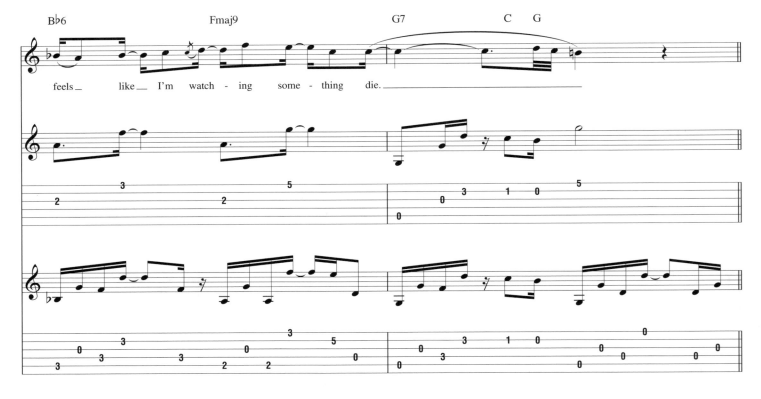

Bb6          Fmaj9                    G7              C     G

feels \_\_ like \_\_ I'm watch - ing some - thing die. _____

**Interlude**
Gtr. 2 tacet
Gm7

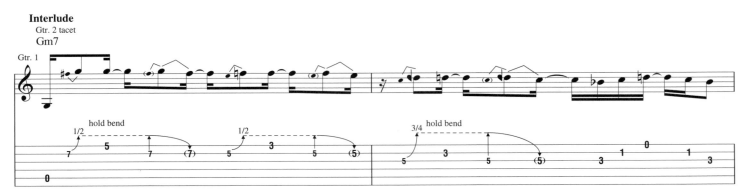

Gtr. 1

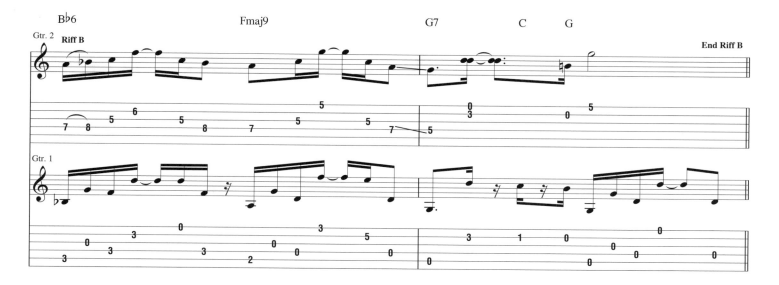

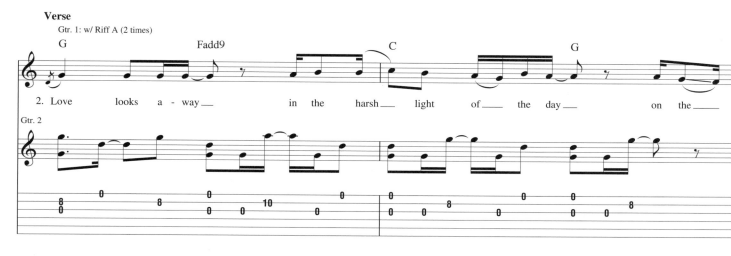

**Verse**

Gtr. 1: w/ Riff A (2 times)

2. Love looks a - way ___ in the harsh ___ light of ___ the day ___ on the ___

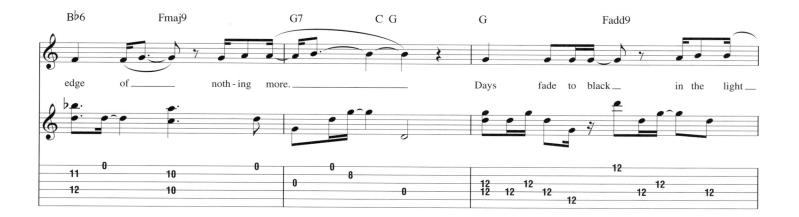

edge of ___ noth - ing more. ___ Days fade to black ___ in the light ___

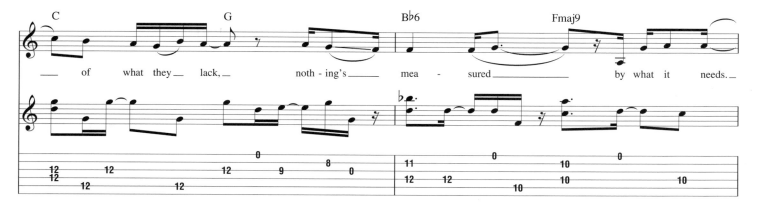

___ of what they ___ lack, ___ noth - ing's ___ mea - sured ___ by what it needs. ___

**Interlude**

Gtr. 2 tacet

Gm7

Gtr. 1

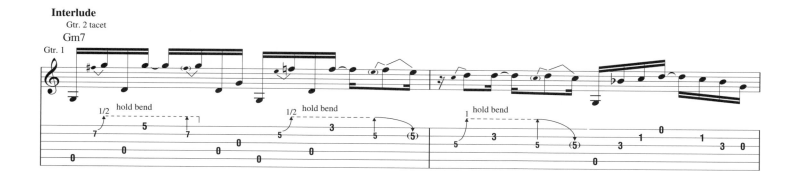

Gtr. 2: w/ Riff B

B♭6                    Fmaj9                    G7              C        G

**Outro**

Gadd11                 Gm11                     Gm(add9)

Gtr. 2

Gtr. 1

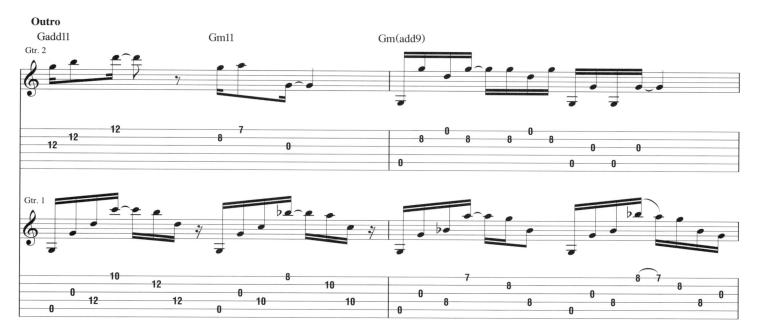

Fmaj11                 Cadd11                   G7              C        G

*poco rit.*

*poco rit.*

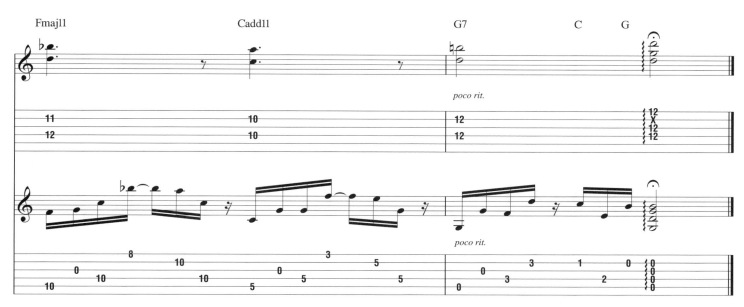

# Sunday Sun

**Words and Music by Beck Hansen**

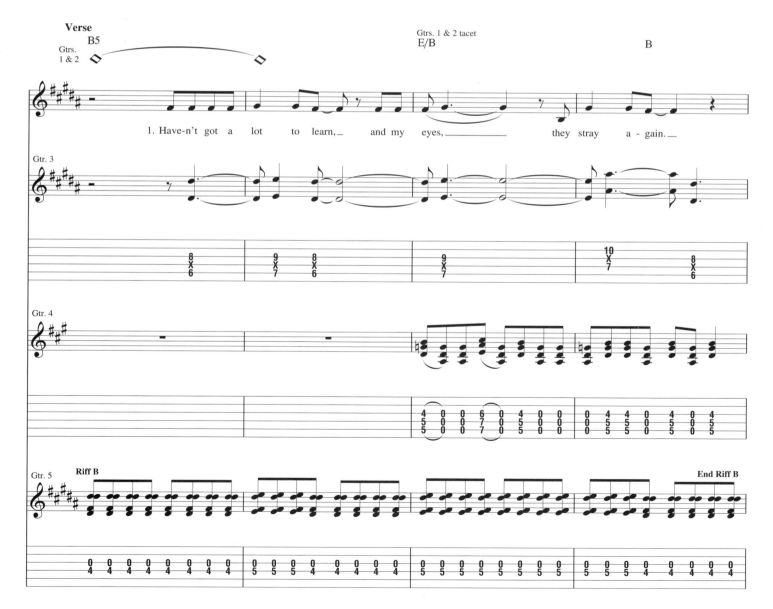

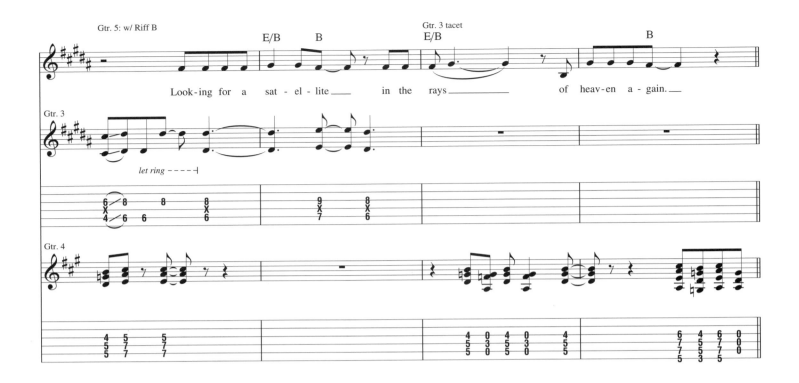

Look-ing for a sat-el-lite ____ in the rays _____ of heav-en a-gain. ____

**Chorus**

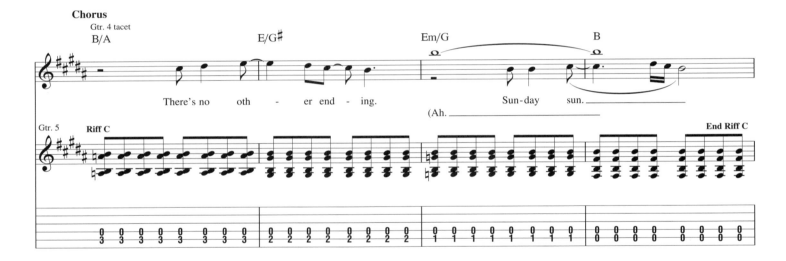

There's no oth - er end - ing. Sun-day sun. ____

(Ah. ____

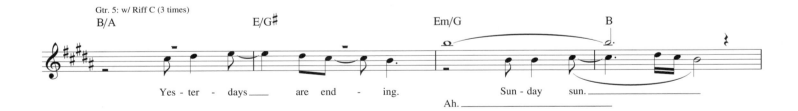

Yes - ter - days ____ are end - ing. Sun - day sun. _____

Ah. ____

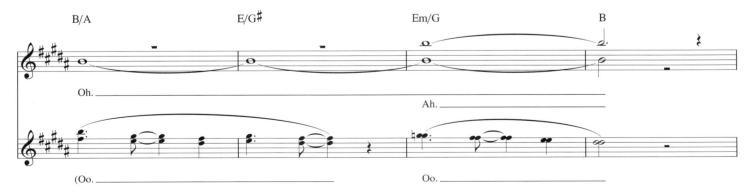

Oh. ____

Ah. ____

(Oo. ____

Oo. ____

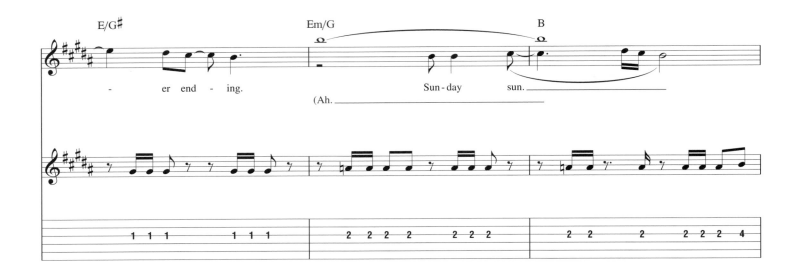

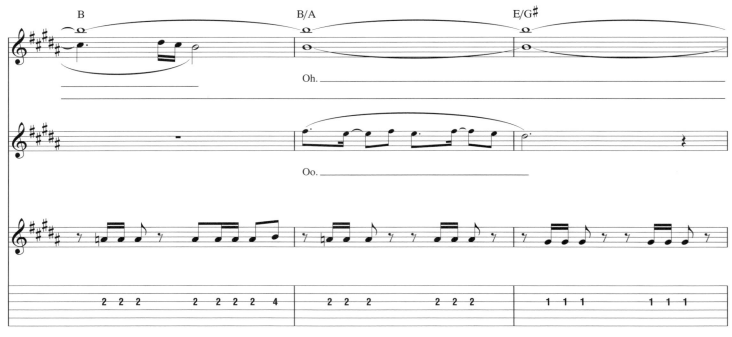

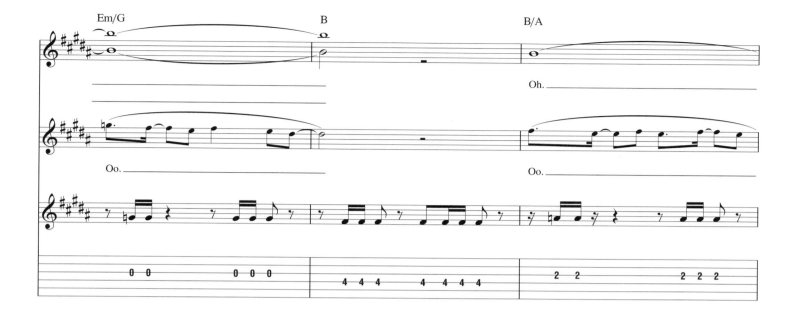

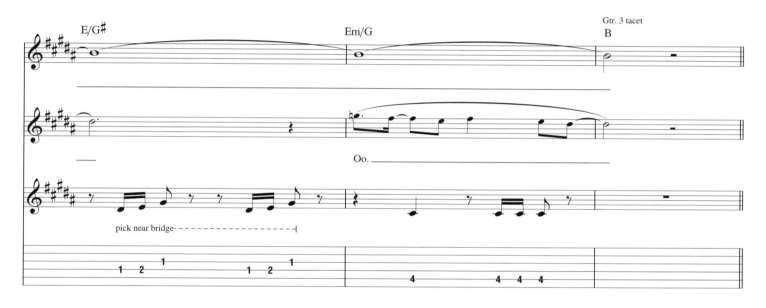

**Interlude**
Gtr. 5: w/ Riff A (2 times)

**Chorus**
Gtr. 5: w/ Riff C (8 times)

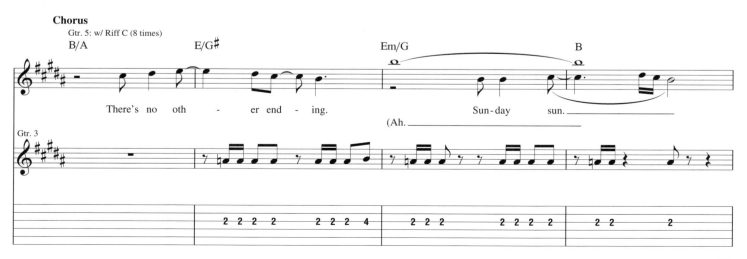

There's no oth- er end- ing.                    Sun-day   sun.

(Ah.

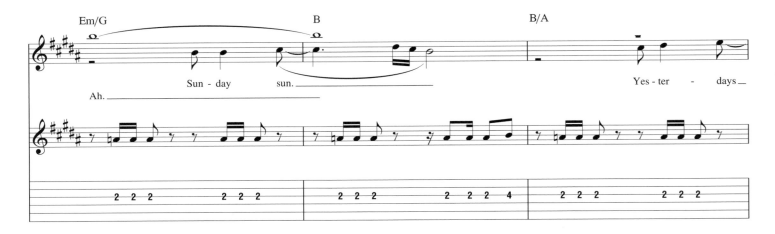

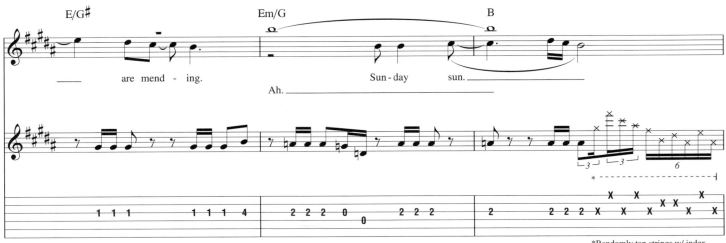

*Randomly tap strings w/ index
and middle finger of R.H.

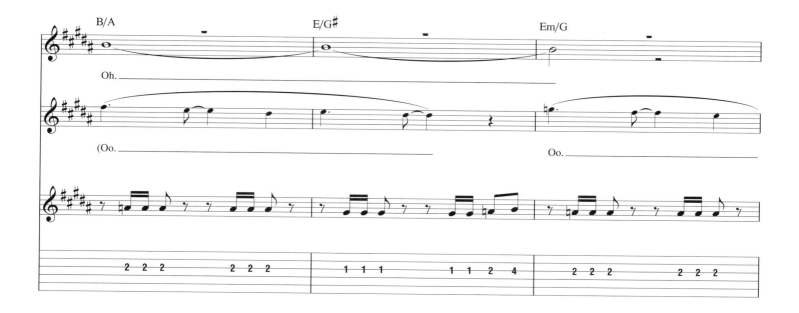

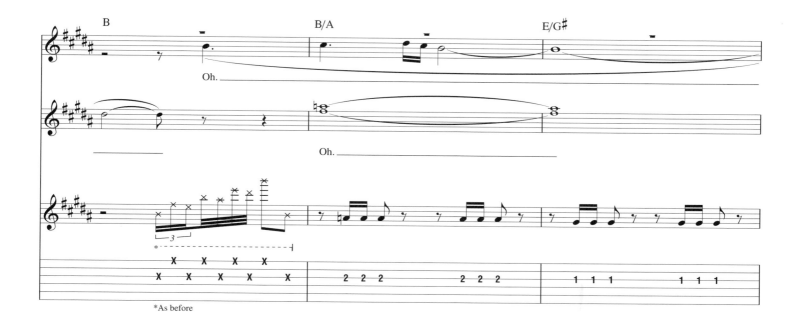

*As before

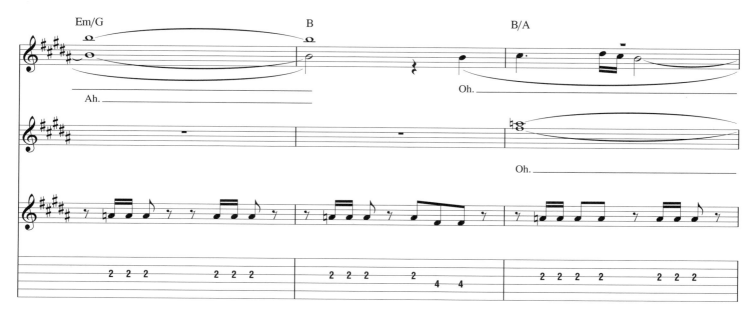

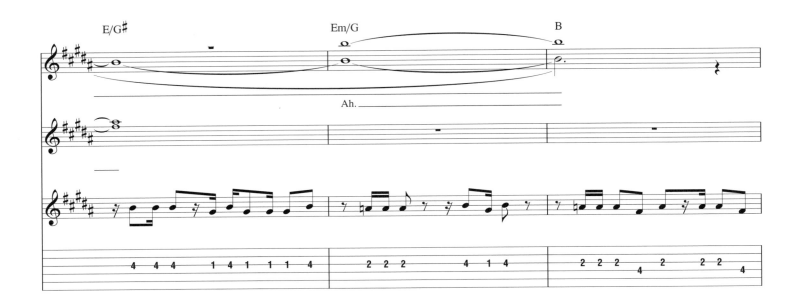

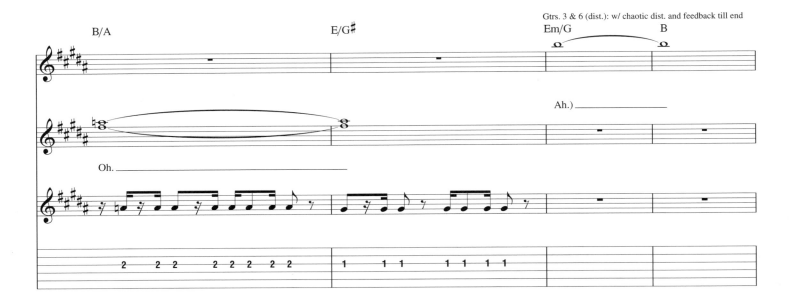

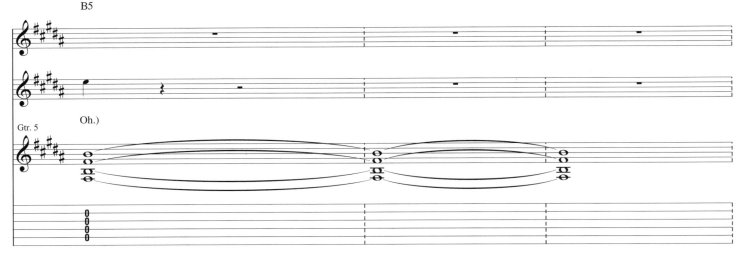

# Little One

**Words and Music by Beck Hansen**

to throw your chains a - way, try to hang your hopes on the wind.

**Chorus**

Lit - tle one, just a lit - tle way. To - day,

*Chord symbols reflect overall harmony.

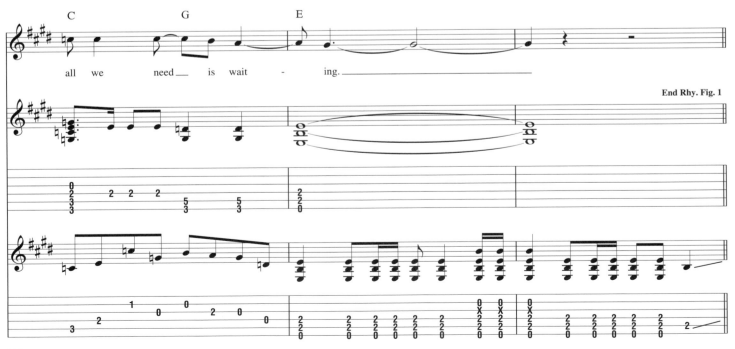

all we need is wait - ing.

End Rhy. Fig. 1

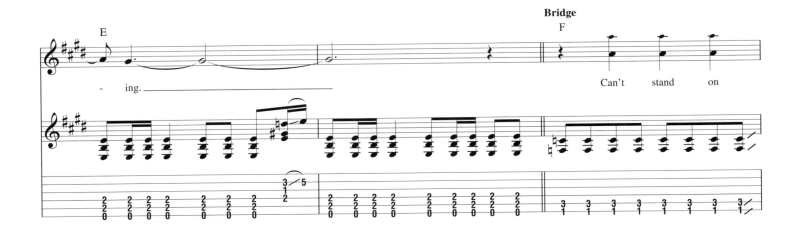

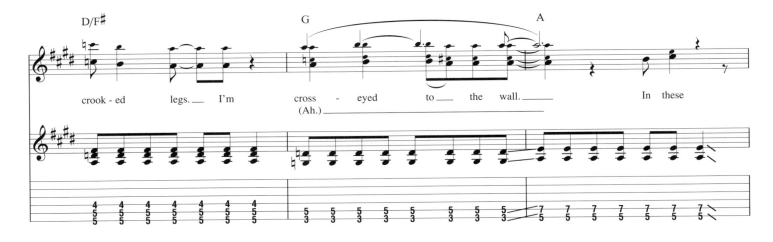

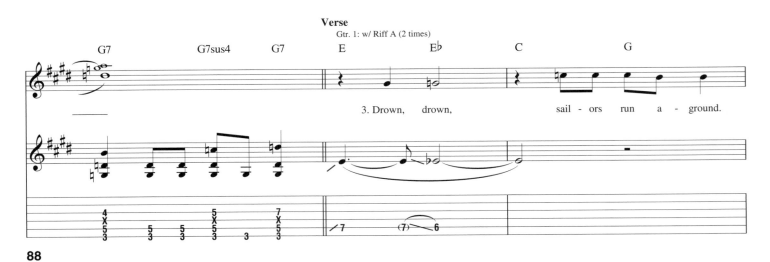

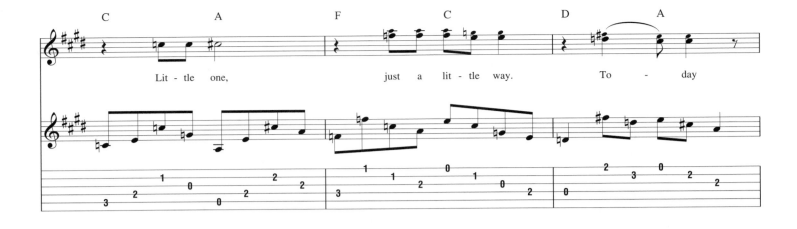

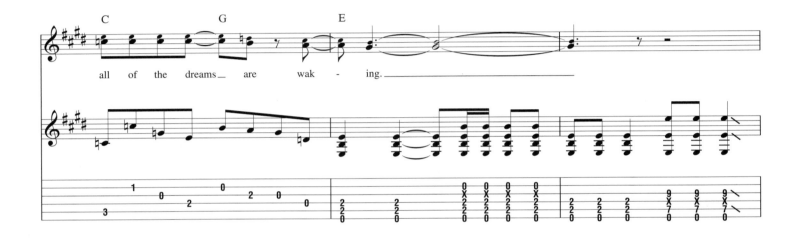

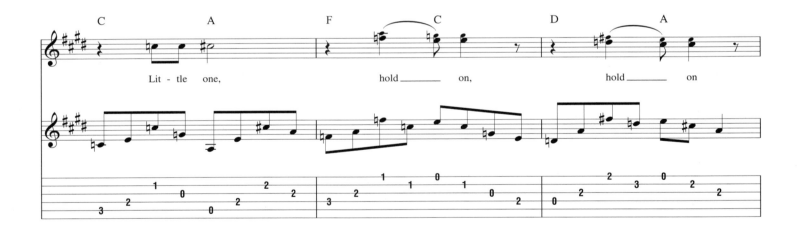

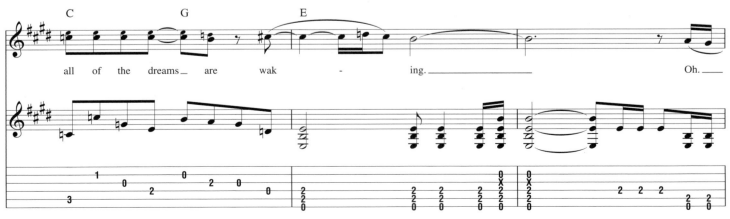

\*Gtr. 4 (clean)

*p*

w/ dist.

\*Two gtrs. arr. for one.

\*\*Gtrs. 2 & 3

\*\*Composite arrangement

Oh.

Oh.

let ring

Oh. _____   Oh. _____

Oh. _____

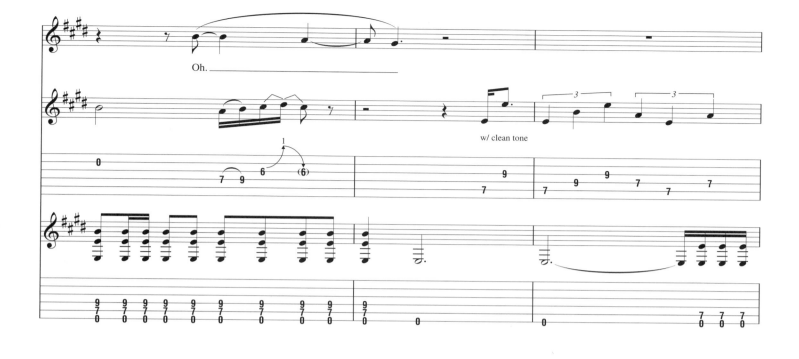

Oh.

w/ clean tone

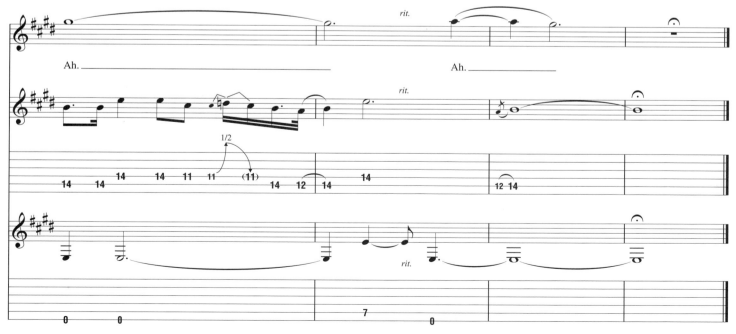

Ah. _____ Ah. _____

rit.

# Side of the Road

### Words and Music by Beck Hansen

Gtr. 1: Open C tuning
(low to high) C-G-C-G-C-E
Gtr. 2: Tuning:
(low to high) C-G-C-E-G-C

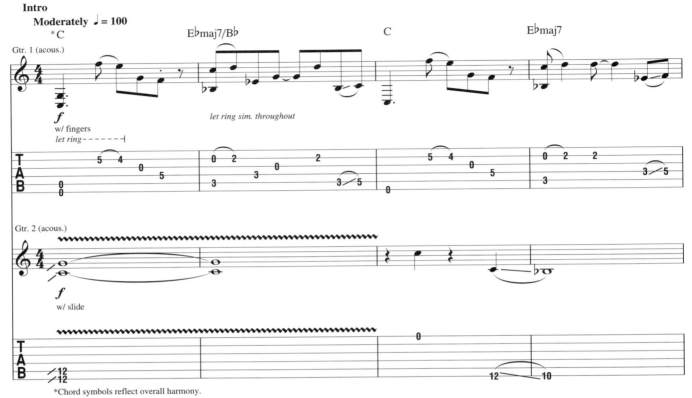

*Chord symbols reflect overall harmony.

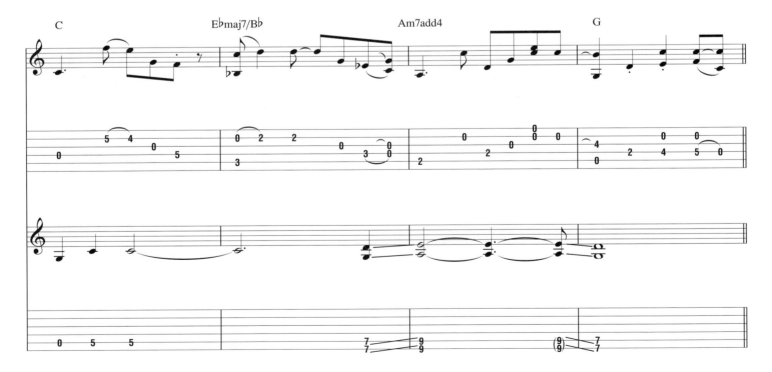

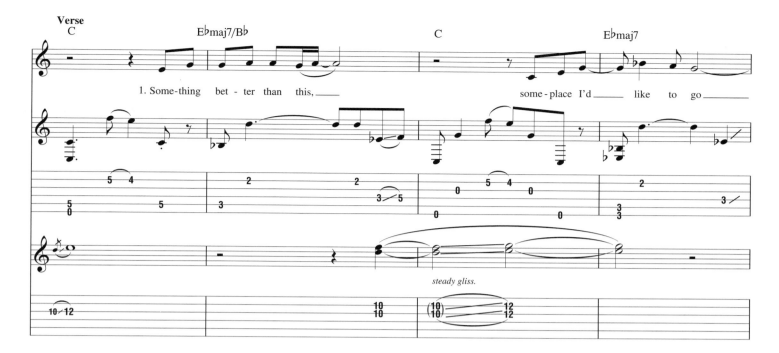

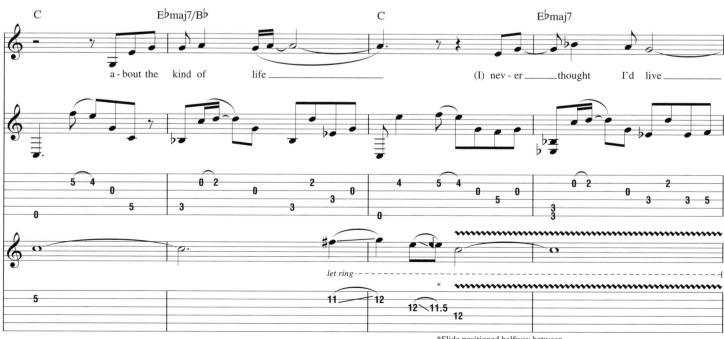

*Slide positioned halfway between
11th & 12th frets.

till the ug-ly truth ____ showed me what it ____ did.

w/ pick & finger

**Chorus**

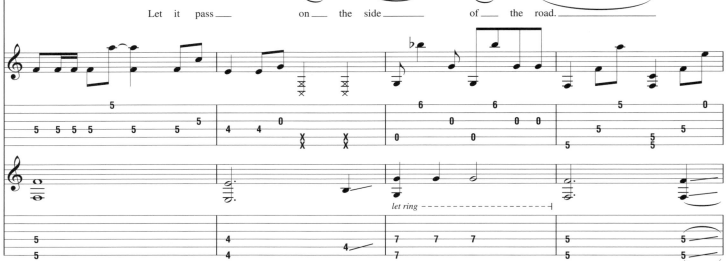

Let it pass ____ on ____ the side ____ of ____ the road. ____

let ring ----------------------

What a friend ____ could tell me now. _____

let ring ------------------------------------

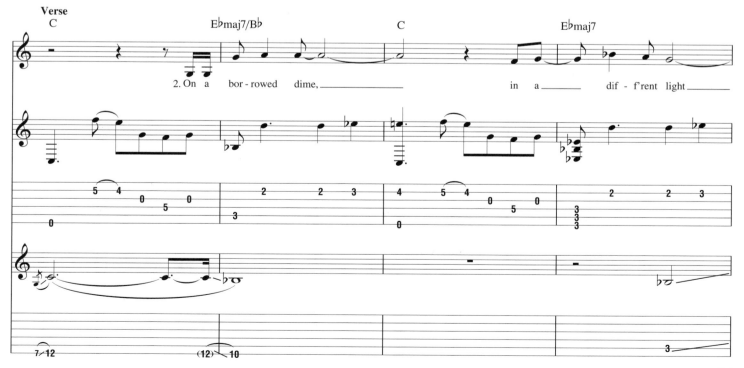

2. On a bor-rowed dime, _____ in a _____ dif-f'rent light _____

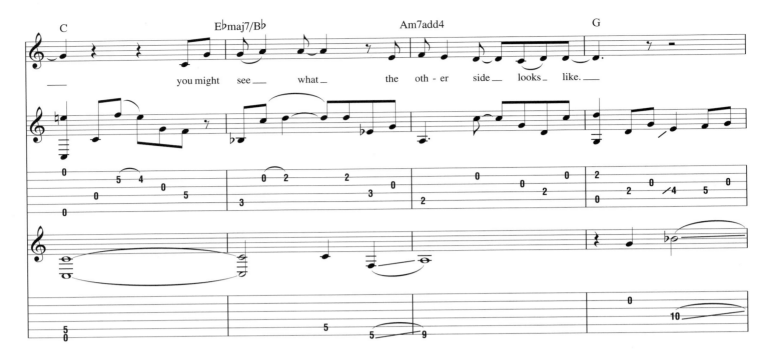

you might see \_\_ what \_\_ the oth-er side looks\_ like. \_\_

In a ran-dom room _____ and an \_\_ i-ron door _____

kick an emp-ty can \_\_ a-cross an emp-ty \_\_ floor. \_\_

**Chorus**

Let it pass on the side of the road

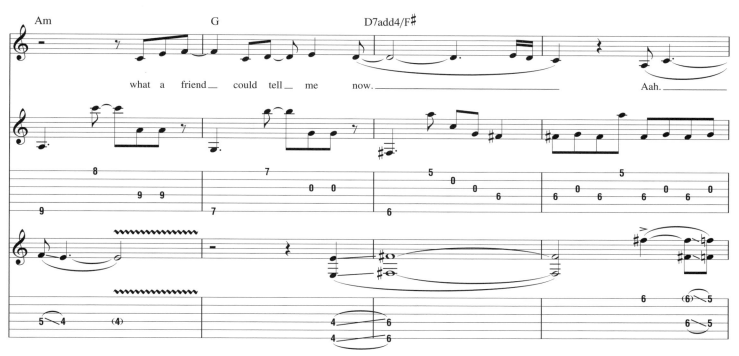

what a friend could tell me now. Aah.

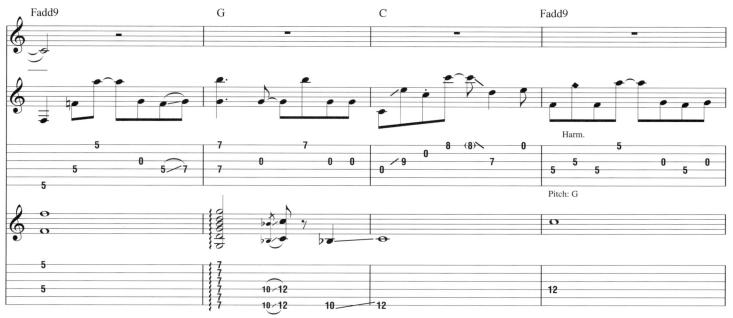

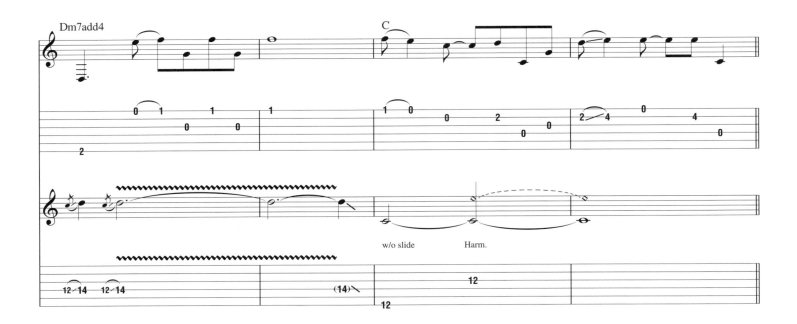

**Outro**

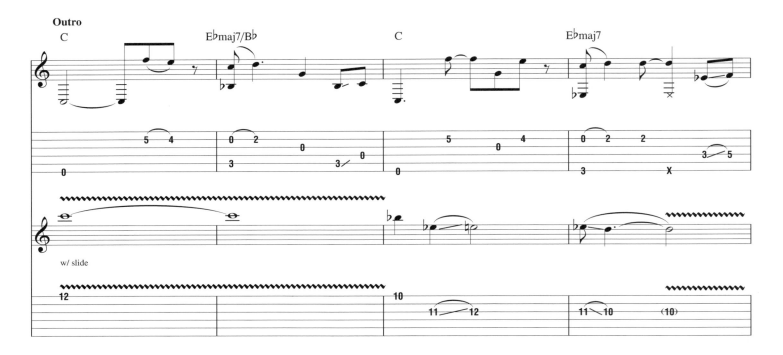

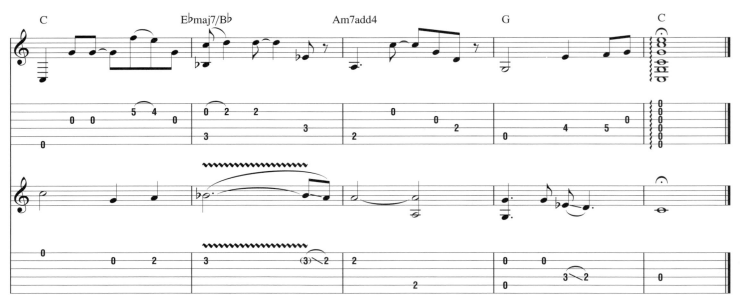

# Guitar Notation Legend

Guitar Music can be notated three different ways: on a *musical staff*, in *tablature*, and in *rhythm slashes*.

**RHYTHM SLASHES** are written above the staff. Strum chords in the rhythm indicated. Use the chord diagrams found at the top of the first page of the transcription for the appropriate chord voicings. Round noteheads indicate single notes.

**THE MUSICAL STAFF** shows pitches and rhythms and is divided by bar lines into measures. Pitches are named after the first seven letters of the alphabet.

**TABLATURE** graphically represents the guitar fingerboard. Each horizontal line represents a a string, and each number represents a fret.

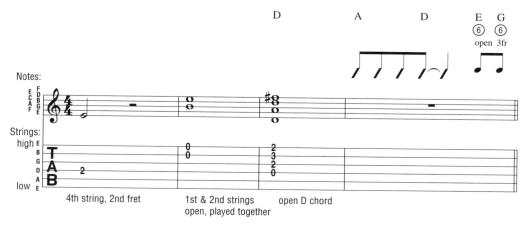

4th string, 2nd fret     1st & 2nd strings open, played together     open D chord

# Definitions for Special Guitar Notation

**HALF-STEP BEND:** Strike the note and bend up 1/2 step.

**WHOLE-STEP BEND:** Strike the note and bend up one step.

**GRACE NOTE BEND:** Strike the note and immediately bend up as indicated.

**SLIGHT (MICROTONE) BEND:** Strike the note and bend up 1/4 step.

**BEND AND RELEASE:** Strike the note and bend up as indicated, then release back to the original note. Only the first note is struck.

**PRE-BEND:** Bend the note as indicated, then strike it.

**PRE-BEND AND RELEASE:** Bend the note as indicated. Strike it and release the bend back to the original note.

**UNISON BEND:** Strike the two notes simultaneously and bend the lower note up to the pitch of the higher.

**VIBRATO:** The string is vibrated by rapidly bending and releasing the note with the fretting hand.

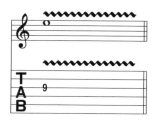

**WIDE VIBRATO:** The pitch is varied to a greater degree by vibrating with the fretting hand.

**HAMMER-ON:** Strike the first (lower) note with one finger, then sound the higher note (on the same string) with another finger by fretting it without picking.

**PULL-OFF:** Place both fingers on the notes to be sounded. Strike the first note and without picking, pull the finger off to sound the second (lower) note.

**LEGATO SLIDE:** Strike the first note and then slide the same fret-hand finger up or down to the second note. The second note is not struck.

**SHIFT SLIDE:** Same as legato slide, except the second note is struck.

**TRILL:** Very rapidly alternate between the notes indicated by continuously hammering on and pulling off.

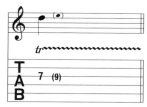

**TAPPING:** Hammer ("tap") the fret indicated with the pick-hand index or middle finger and pull off to the note fretted by the fret hand.

**NATURAL HARMONIC:** Strike the note while the fret-hand lightly touches the string directly over the fret indicated.

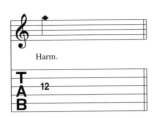

Harm.

**PINCH HARMONIC:** The note is fretted normally and a harmonic is produced by adding the edge of the thumb or the tip of the index finger of the pick hand to the normal pick attack.

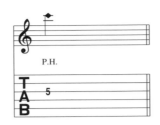

P.H.

**HARP HARMONIC:** The note is fretted normally and a harmonic is produced by gently resting the pick hand's index finger directly above the indicated fret (in parentheses) while the pick hand's thumb or pick assists by plucking the appropriate string.

H.H.

**PICK SCRAPE:** The edge of the pick is rubbed down (or up) the string, producing a scratchy sound.

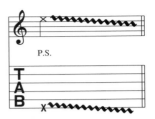

P.S.

**MUFFLED STRINGS:** A percussive sound is produced by laying the fret hand across the string(s) without depressing, and striking them with the pick hand.

**PALM MUTING:** The note is partially muted by the pick hand lightly touching the string(s) just before the bridge.

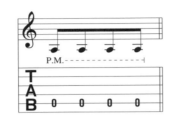

P.M.

**RAKE:** Drag the pick across the strings indicated with a single motion.

rake

**TREMOLO PICKING:** The note is picked as rapidly and continuously as possible.

**ARPEGGIATE:** Play the notes of the chord indicated by quickly rolling them from bottom to top.

**VIBRATO BAR DIVE AND RETURN:** The pitch of the note or chord is dropped a specified number of steps (in rhythm) then returned to the original pitch.

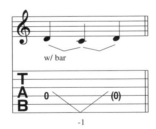

w/ bar

**VIBRATO BAR SCOOP:** Depress the bar just before striking the note, then quickly release the bar.

w/ bar

**VIBRATO BAR DIP:** Strike the note and then immediately drop a specified number of steps, then release back to the original pitch.

w/ bar

# Additional Musical Definitions

| | | |
|---|---|---|
| (accent) | • Accentuate note (play it louder) | |
| (accent) | • Accentuate note with great intensity | |
| (staccato) | • Play the note short | |
| | • Downstroke | |
| | • Upstroke | |
| **D.S. al Coda** | • Go back to the sign ( % ), then play until the measure marked "*To Coda*," then skip to the section labelled "*Coda*." | |
| **D.C. al Fine** | • Go back to the beginning of the song and play until the measure marked "*Fine*" (end). | |

| | |
|---|---|
| **Rhy. Fig.** | • Label used to recall a recurring accompaniment pattern (usually chordal). |
| **Riff** | • Label used to recall composed, melodic lines (usually single notes) which recur. |
| **Fill** | • Label used to identify a brief melodic figure which is to be inserted into the arrangement. |
| **Rhy. Fill** | • A chordal version of a Fill. |
| **tacet** | • Instrument is silent (drops out). |
| | • Repeat measures between signs. |
| 1. 2. | • When a repeated section has different endings, play the first ending only the first time and the second ending only the second time. |

**NOTE:**  Tablature numbers in parentheses mean:
1. The note is being sustained over a system (note in standard notation is tied), or
2. The note is sustained, but a new articulation (such as a hammer-on, pull-off, slide or vibrato begins), or
3. The note is a barely audible "ghost" note (note in standard notation is also in parentheses).